A garden house at Hidcote, Gloucestershire. Made between 1905 and 1939, Hidcote was the first garden to be accepted, in 1948, by the National Trust's Gardens Committee. This opened a new era in the appreciation of garden design as a fine art.

ENGLISH GARDEN DESIGN

History and styles since 1650

Tom Turner

Antique Collectors' Club

ISBN 0 907462 25 1

British Library CIP data

Turner, Tom
    English garden design: history and
    styles since 1650
    1. Landscape gardening — England —
    History
    I. Title
    712'.6'0942   SB466.G7

Published for the Antique Collectors' Club
by the Antique Collectors' Club Ltd

Printed in England by the Antique Collectors' Club, Woodbridge, Suffolk

Contents

Preface   7

Chapter I   English Garden Design: The Background Ideas   9

Chapter II   1650-1740: The Enclosed, French and Dutch Styles   44

Chapter III   1714-1810: The Forest, Serpentine and Irregular Styles   74

Chapter IV   1794-1870: The Transition, Italian and Mixed Styles   113

Chapter V   1870-1985: The Arts and Crafts and Abstract Styles;   166
                 Recent Trends

References and Notes   228

Select Bibliography   233

Index   234

To the memory of H.F. Clark

Preface

Frank Clark, who wrote a most charming book, *The English Landscape Garden*, was once asked to give evidence at a public inquiry about the value of preserving an eighteenth century garden through which the Ministry of Transport wished to run a motorway. Ill health prevented him from attending, but he told his students he had been ready to claim that the ideas which led to the design of such gardens represented a more important English contribution to western culture than either Shakespeare's plays or Milton's poetry. His reasoning was simple: many countries have produced great poets but England is the only country to have produced a complete theory of outdoor design. The first application of the theory was to gardens but, as Christopher Hussey tells in *The Picturesque,* it subsequently had a dramatic impact on the other arts, ranging from poetry itself, to painting, literature, architecture and town planning. David Watkin has enlarged upon Hussey's discussion of the subject in his book *The English Vision.*

The first chapter of this book gives an account of the ideas on which the art of garden design was based in England. The remaining chapters describe and illustrate the various styles which have resulted from these ideas. Dates are given for the period covered by each chapter — they are arbitrary but help to describe the contents. Eleven styles of garden design are named and illustrated in the course of the book. Some are well represented by surviving examples, others very poorly. Where appropriate I have used old engravings and photographs to illustrate more accurately the intentions of the original garden designers.

The care of historic gardens has become an important sphere of activity for landscape architects and, though many of these gardens are at risk through neglect, many restorations are in hand. I would like to make a personal plea for some restoration projects which would be of special historical value as examples of poorly represented styles: the semi-circular parterre which should lie in front of Hampton Court; the great flight of grass steps in Greenwich Park; London and Wise's parterre at Melbourne Hall, Derbyshire; the *fermes ornées* at The Leasowes and Great Tew; and some full-scale Gertrude Jekyll borders with colour schemes based on J.M.W. Turner's colour theory. Munstead would be an ideal location but others could be made in several urban parks and in gardens which are open to the public.

Although the title of this book refers to English garden design, some of the designers are not English and a few of the examples are in Scotland and Wales. English is used in preference to British because it describes a culture rather than an empire.

I am grateful to Professor G.P. Henderson who introduced me to the philosophy of aesthetics, and to Frank Clark who aroused my interest in the history of garden design and lent me his copy of A.O. Lovejoy's *The Great Chain of Being,* a work which has had a considerable influence on this book. I hope to have acknowledged my intellectual debts in the text.

I would also like to thank Michael Lancaster and my wife, Margaret, for continuous advice on the manuscript, Adam Czerniawski for advice on the first chapter, and Cherry Lewis for her careful editorial work. Individuals and organisations who kindly gave permission to reproduce illustrations are acknowledged in the captions. Other photographs and drawings are mine or my wife's.

The Garden of Eden as shown on the frontispiece to the most popular seventeenth century book on English garden plants: John Parkinson's Paridisi in Sole Paradisus Terrestris, *1629. The inscription at the top of the page is the Hebrew name of God and the French poem at the bottom of the page proclaims: 'Whoever wants to compare Art with Nature and our parks with Eden, indiscreetly measures the stride of the elephant by the stride of the mite and the flight of the eagle by that of the gnat'.*

CHAPTER I

English Garden Design: The Background Ideas

One of the great divides in the history of English garden design is marked by the Civil War of 1642-9. No gardens survive from before the War, and after it garden designers were subject to a range of influences which brought about a dynamic period of stylistic development — and the creation of several uniquely English styles of garden and landscape design. The War and its associated troubles also caused proprietors to reconsider the objectives of garden design. They came to see their estates less as backgrounds to social events and more as places of secure retreat from the dangers of political and religious strife. In so doing they looked back to an older tradition deriving from Christian theology as well as from Roman and Greek philosophy which celebrated the garden as a place in which use could be combined with beauty, profit with pleasure, and work with contemplation.

The first element of the gardening ideal to take root in England came from the biblical account of the Fall. The Book of Genesis recounts the story as follows:

> And the Lord God planted a garden eastward in Eden; and there he put the man whom he had formed. And out of the ground made the Lord God to grow every tree that is pleasant to the sight; and good for food; and the tree of life also in the midst of the garden, and the tree of knowledge of good and evil. . . And the Lord God took the man and put him into the garden of Eden to dress it and keep it.[1]

But Adam and Eve disobeyed God's command and ate of the tree of knowledge of good and evil:

> And unto Adam he said, Because thou has hearkened unto the voice of thy wife, and has eaten of the tree, of which I commanded thee, saying, Thou shalt not eat of it: cursed is the ground for thy sake: in sorrow shalt thou eat of it all the days of thy life; Thorns also and thistles shall it bring forth to thee; and thou shalt eat the herb of the field; In the sweat of thy face shalt thou eat bread, till thou return unto the ground: for dust thou art, and unto dust shalt thou return.[2]

The biblical story of Adam and Eve in the garden of Eden and their banishment from it, makes the point that man was charged with horticultural duties both before and after his fall from grace. Before his expulsion from paradise he was required to 'dress and keep' the garden of Eden. After the Fall he was condemned to cultivate the ground 'in the sweat of thy face' and to 'eat the herb of the field'. A distinction has been drawn between the pleasurable task of tending a garden and the onerous task of eking a living from ground which is strewn with thorns and thistles.

It therefore appeared to Christian thinkers that gardening was not only one of the purest and most divine activities open to man, it was also a way of recreating the paradise which man had once shared with God.

This consideration was deeply felt by Christian monks who devoted their lives

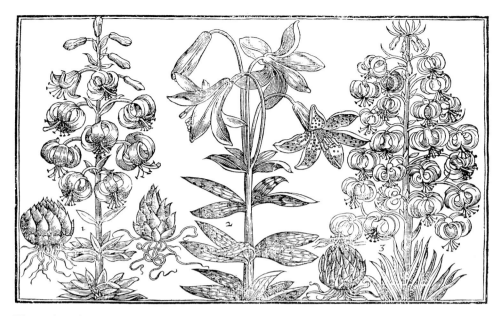

Illustrations for the lily, above, and rose, right, from Parkinson's Paradisi in Sole Paradisus Terrestris, *1629. The two flowers have long had strong devotional associations — the original meaning of 'rosary' being a rose garden.*

to a routine of prayer and manual work. Monastic gardens provided fruit and vegetables for the kitchen, herbs for the hospital and flowers with which to decorate altars and shrines. The original meaning of 'rosary' was a rose garden and the most widely grown devotional flowers were the rose and the lily. In some monasteries each monk had a private garden attached to his cell which could be used for cultivating flowers, fruit and vegetables.

The monastic gardening tradition, brought to England with the Norman conquest, had a pervasive influence on medieval gardens both as an attitude to gardening and as a source of scientific knowledge, though during the sixteenth and seventeenth centuries it was overlaid by Renaissance gardening ideas.

The rural retirement theme in Rome and Greece

During the sixteenth and seventeenth centuries the Renaissance had a vast impact on English culture. It was natural that writers on gardening and agriculture should join with their scholarly contemporaries in looking to Italy for artistic and scientific knowledge. They looked both to Renaissance authors, such as Alberti, Palladio and Colonna, as well as to their Roman predecessors, including Virgil, Horace, Vitruvius, Pliny and Columella. For practical advice the best sources were Virgil's *Georgics* and Columella's *De Re Rustica*. English writers on gardening found that these two works contained a wealth of advice on rural topics, including tillage, agricultural tools, raising trees, pruning, caring for animals and the management of bees. Columella loved country life and believed that agriculture is 'without doubt most closely related to and, as it were, own sister to wisdom'.[3]

Virgil also delights in practicalities but, though 'Georgic' means 'relating to agriculture', it was not the poet's sole purpose to write an agricultural treatise in verse. His aims were also political and philosophical. Like Horace, his contemporary in first century B.C. Rome, Virgil delighted in the life style of rural retirement. The two poets contrast the virtues of pastoral life with the civil war, waste and political turmoil which plagued Rome after the assassination of Caesar in 44 B.C. They dreamed of a new Golden Age embodying the virtues of peace, productivity and continuity. In particular they pointed to the life style of what

'Blest too is he who knows the rural gods...' These words from Virgil's Georgics *characterise the 'rural retirement' theme which so appealed in seventeenth century England, beset as it was by the Civil War and its associated troubles. The woodcut, from Sebastian Brant's 1502 edition of the* Georgics *(Book IV), shows 'happy husbandmen' tending bees.*
Courtesy The British Library.

Maren-Sofie Røstvig has called 'the happy husbandsman'.[4] His life was one of rural retirement and peaceful toil, free from the temptations of money, power and political advancement. The *Georgics* often return to this theme:

> Blest too is he who knows the rural gods... never pitied he
> Him that hath not, nor envied him that hath.
> What fruits the branches, what the willing earth
> Freely afford, he gathers, nor beholds
> State archives, ruthless laws and city broils.
> Others may vex the treacherous firth with oars
> And rush upon the sword; through palaces
> And courts of kings their headlong course they hold...
> Meantime the husbandman with crooked plough
> Has cleft the earth: hence labour's yearly meed,
> Hence feeds he little child and father land.
> Hence are milch-cow and honest ox maintained.
> Earth never rests: either with fruit she flows,
> Or with young lambs, or with the wheaten sheaf
> Beloved of Ceres: increase the drills
> And barns are overcome.[5]

Although Virgil and Horace are among the greatest poets to have praised the virtues of rural retirement they were not the originators of the theme. The

Following the upheavals and conflicts of the Civil War, and the subsequent persecution of first Protestants, and then Catholics, seventeenth and eighteenth century England saw many landowners retreating to their country estates and extolling the virtues of 'rural retirement', which was peaceful, safer, and more profitable than town life. This attitude had a profound influence on the development of garden design.

peacefulness of rural life was a favourite topic of the Greek poets, such as Homer and Theocritus, on whom Virgil and Horace modelled their poetry. In Greece philosophy had long been associated with gardens.[6] Horace studied at the academy in Athens as a young man and may have been taught philosophy in the garden, as had been the custom of Plato and Epicurus. He particularly admired Epicurus' doctrine that happiness results from the enjoyments of the mind and the sweets of virtue. When he was offered the job of private secretary to Augustus he turned it down because he liked best the life of rural retirement on his farm in the Sabine Hills:

> Happy the man who bounteous Gods allow,
> With his own hands Paternal Grounds to plough.[7]

There he could live among happy husbandmen with cheerful faces engaged in cultivating the vine, shearing lambs, gathering fruit, ploughing the soil and looking after bees.

The rural retirement theme in England

During the seventeenth century England suffered from civil war and political upheaval on a scale which could be compared to the troubles which had afflicted Rome in the first century B.C. The English troubles, which centred on the conflict between the Royalists and Parliamentarians, led to a greater appreciation of country life. As in Roman times, rural retirement appeared both safer and more virtuous than living in town. During Charles I's reign many of the Protestants, who later formed the core of the Parliamentarians, were unjustly persecuted. After the outbreak of the Civil War, in 1642, both parties suffered.

The execution of Charles I in 1649 brought the war to an end and Cromwell exiled the defeated Royalists to the country. Here, they made a virtue of necessity and devoted themselves to agriculture and the improvement of their estates. The Commonwealth survived until 1660 and ended with the Restoration of the monarchy in the person of Charles II. A new period of religious and political persecution began with the execution of the regicides who had been responsible for beheading Charles I. It was now the turn of Protestant landowners to find life safest in their country retreats. John Milton, the poet and apologist for the Commonwealth, himself retired into the country for a time after the Restoration and began work on *Paradise Lost*. Book IV contains a description of the Garden of Eden before the Fall. It was frequently quoted by eighteenth century poets and gardening authors, and contains the following lines which compare Eden to a rural estate:

> Thus was this place,
> A happy rural seat of various view;
> Groves whose rich Trees wept odorous Gumms and Balme,
> Others whose fruit burnisht with Golden Rinde...
> Betwixt them Lawns, or level Downs, and Flocks
> Grasing the tender herb, were interpos'd,
> Or palmie hilloc, or the flourie lap
> Of som irriguous Valley spread her store.[8]

The persecution of Protestants reached a climax between 1685 and 1688 and led directly to the Glorious Revolution of 1688 and the invitation to the Protestant

William of Orange to assume the English throne. It was, once again, the turn of the Catholics to find life safer away from the court and town.

By the end of the seventeenth century writers on many subjects, but especially writers on gardening, were praising the ideal of rural retirement. They looked to Renaissance authors for practical advice but were also attracted to the life style which they praised. William Temple exemplifies this attitude. He was a Protestant diplomat and statesman who from 1655 to 1680 had been through stormy times. The crowning achievement of his career was the negotiation, in 1668, of the Triple Alliance of Protestant countries to protect Holland from Catholic aggression. This was no mean feat since Charles II, had strong French and Catholic sympathies. To Temple's regret, however, the Alliance came to nothing. Towards the end of his career he was offered a secretaryship of state but he was weary of political strife and declined the offer. In true Horatian style he retired to a rural seat at Sheen, Richmond-upon-Thames, and devoted himself to estate management and

Above, the Garden of Eden as illustrated in a 1688 edition of Milton's Paradise Lost. *Above right, an illustration of rural husbandry from a 1774 edition of Virgil's* Georgics *(Book III).* Courtesy The British Library.

literature; his essay of 1685 *Upon the Gardens of Epicurus* extols his country refuge:

> The sweetness and satisfaction of this retreat, where since my resolution taken of never entering again into any public employments, I have passed five years without once going to town, though I am almost in sight of it, and have a house there always ready to receive me.[9]

Temple enormously admired the Greek philosopher whose name appears in the title of his essay:

> Epicurus passed his life wholly in his garden: there he studied, there he exercised, there he taught his philosophy . . . [because] the sweetness of air, the pleasantness of smell, the verdure of plants, the cleanness and lightness of food, the exercises of working and walking; but above all, the exemption from cares and solicitude, seem equally to favour and improve both contemplation and health.[10]

Temple's idea of a garden was as traditional as his gardening philosophy. His own garden, Moor Park, Surrey, which will be described in the next chapter, had a series of walled and hedged rectangular enclosures which were devoted to flowers, vegetables and fruit — he was especially interested in the latter. His essay is by no means a pomological treatise but, following the *Georgics,* contains practical advice distilled from the author's personal experience.

Anthony Ashley Cooper, third Earl of Shaftesbury, is another writer who praised the joys of rural life. The two friends who conduct a debate in his 'philosophical rhapsody' *The Moralists,* set out for a walk and 'fell naturally into the praises of country life, and discoursed a while of husbandry, and the nature of the soil'.[11] They proceed to a discussion of nature, ethics and aesthetics. Shaftesbury believed that a garden should induce peacefulness and spirituality:

> Therefore remember ever the garden and the groves within. There build, there erect what statues, what virtues, what ornament or orders of architecture thou thinkest noblest. There walk at leisure and in peace; contemplate, regulate, dispose: and for this, a bare field or common walk will serve full as well, and to say truth, much better.[12]

Stephen Switzer is a third example of a gardening author who was influenced by the classical idea of rural retirement. He published his first book in 1715 but his philosophy is basically that of the previous century. Switzer is careful to acknowledge his sources and begins with the Garden of Eden. Epicurus is credited with making the first town garden and praised for using it as a place to teach philosophy. Virgil is admired for the way he 'mixes the poet, philosopher and gardener together'.[13] The art of choosing a good site and planning the layout is properly ascribed to Vitruvius. John Evelyn is seen as a second Virgil on account of his grasp of the technical and philosophical aspects of country life and, among other writers, Switzer mentions Homer, Horace, Columella, Ovid, Milton, Cowley, Temple, Addison and Pope. He also gives grateful thanks to his former employers, London and Wise, and to the French designers and authors who provided the model for his work. In the course of a long apprenticeship Switzer had learnt more about the practicalities of estate work than Temple or Shaftesbury had ever known. He was a nurseryman and designer who sought to combine 'the pleasures of the country with the profits'.[14]

Portrait of Sir William Temple by Sir Peter Lely.
Courtesy The National Portrait Gallery.

Although Temple, Shaftesbury and Switzer have been taken as representative gardening authors of their period, and have been shown to embrace an ancient gardening ideal, it must also be said that these men are best known to historians as the precursors of those who developed a uniquely English style of garden and estate layout which arose during the eighteenth century. This style, which is known variously as the 'natural', 'irregular', 'informal' or 'English landscape', contrasts very markedly with the 'geometrical', 'regular' or 'formal' styles which characterised the gardens of the seventeenth century. Pevsner only expressed a popular judgement rather boldly when he wrote of the last passage* of Temple's essay:

> This passage is one of the most amazing in the English language. It started a line of thought and visual conceptions which were to dominate first England and then the World for two centuries. It is the first suggestion ever of a possible beauty fundamentally different from the formal, a beauty of irregularity and fancy.[15]

Similarly Shaftesbury is described by Burke as 'the first philosophical sponsor of a new movement in gardening',[16] and Switzer, by Hunt and Willis, as 'the first professional gardener in England to write about the new style'.[17]

Prophets of a new style?

To what extent did Temple, Shaftesbury and Switzer really support the new English style? At first sight it is puzzling that they should be so widely believed to have done so.

Switzer was trained in the French and Dutch Styles by London and Wise. He

*In which Temple wrote: 'There may be other forms wholly irregular, that may, for aught I know, have more beauty... They must owe it... to some great race of fancy or judgement in the contrivance'.

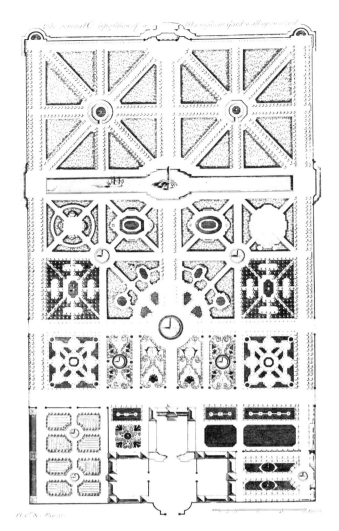

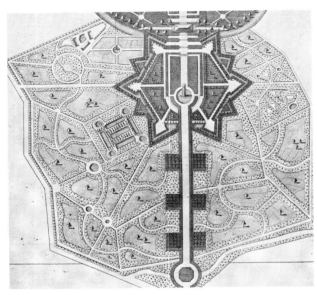

Switzer's design for 'The Manor of Paston' as illustrated in Ichnographia Rustica. *He wrote: 'Thus may a Planter have all the Walks extending from the interior Parts of his Design plow'd, sow'd, and planted . . . by which means, the* Utile *is mix'd with the* Dulce *in (I hope) a very agreeable manner'* (Vol. III, p.93-4).

An illustration from D'Argenville's book La Théorie et la Pratique du Jardinage, *1709, translated in English 1712.*

greatly admired D'Argenville's book on French gardening practice[18] and, with Versailles in mind, wrote of Louis XIV: ''Tis certain that gardening was by his means brought to the most magnificent height and splendour imaginable'.[19] Switzer also saw himself as the first English author, rather than mere translator, to advocate the French style in England.[20] Can it really be that Switzer was mistaken in thinking himself an advocate of the geometrical French style? Or are we mistaken in thinking him an advocate of the new English style?

A similar puzzle arises in connection with Shaftesbury. His writings have always been considered a major influence on the English style, but the fine garden, which he described the year before his death, is plainly Italian or French. Writing from Naples, Shaftesbury praises:

> The disposition and order of one of their finer sort of gardens or villas: the kind of harmony to the eye from the various shapes and colours agreeably mixed and ranged in lines intercrossing without confusion and fortunately coincident; a parterre, cypresses, groves, wilderness, walks; statues here and there . . . with all those symmetries that silently express such order, peace, and sweetness'.[21]

It has sometimes been thought that when Shaftesbury wrote of 'the formal mockery of princely gardens' he was mocking the 'formal' style of these gardens, but he criticised such gardens only when they were a substitute for peace and harmony in the minds of their owners. In the same passage he speaks rhetorically

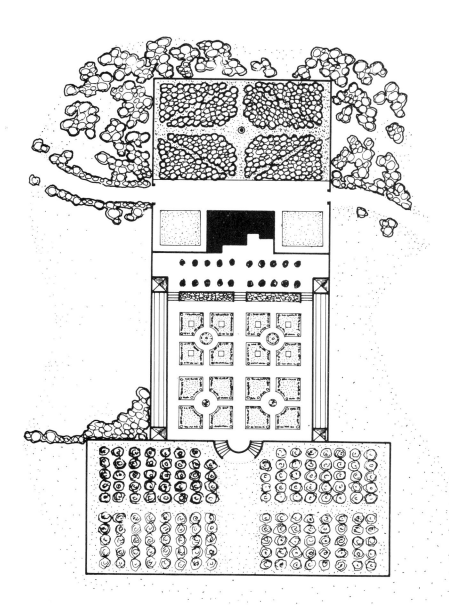

Reconstruction of the plan of the garden at Moor Park, Hertfordshire (pp. 47 and 49). *It is formal and geometric and was described by Temple as 'the perfectest figure of a garden I ever saw', though he has since 1712 been hailed as one of the prophets of a new style.*

Moor Park, Hertfordshire. This is the site of the garden which Temple admired. The original house and garden have gone. They were replaced with a Palladian house, and a garden by Lancelot Brown which is now a golf course.

of 'a coach, liveries, parterre and knolls? cascades, jettes d'eau? — how many rattles?' Shaftesbury thought that grand gardens and all worldly possessions were unimportant 'rattles', and asks 'how can the rational mind rest here, or be satisfied with the absurd enjoyment which reaches the sense alone?'[22] His conception of a fine garden was, however, as geometrical as Switzer's. A careful study of Shaftesbury's own garden at Wimborne St. Giles in Dorset reaches the conclusion that it was based on geometry, perspective and the principle of bringing out the 'intrinsic character' of natural forms. Shaftesbury gave his gardeners the following instruction for dealing with the plantations on the lower canal at Wimbourne St. Giles: 'Every other elm to be taken away and in their place the remaining elms being cut into globes in imitation of ye globe yews on ye same line as the upper canal'.[23]

The puzzle also arises with Temple. He has been hailed as one of the prophets of a new style since 1712, but the garden he describes as 'the perfectest figure of a garden I ever saw' is exceedingly formal and geometric. This garden (Moor Park in Hertfordshire, plan p.17) and Temple's own garden (Moor Park, Surrey), which was also geometric, will be described in the next chapter (pp.47 and 49, and pp.66 and 68-72 respectively).

Before considering a solution to the riddle of why, in the face of the evidence which has been adduced, Temple, Shaftesbury and Switzer are believed to be prophets of a new style, we must examine in more detail the reasons which have been advanced to support the proposition.

The first reason which is given for Temple's originality is his remark that there may be other forms of gardens which are 'wholly irregular'. Shaftesbury and Switzer join in the praise of irregularity. Shaftesbury refers to 'all the horrid graces of the wilderness itself, as representing nature more'',[24] and Switzer to 'the beauty of rural and extensive gardening, when compared with the stiff Dutch way'.[25] But the English taste for irregularity was not new at the end of the seventeenth century. Wooton had stated much more explicity in 1624 that a garden 'should be irregular',[26] and Bacon had written in 1625 that he would like part of his garden to be a 'natural wilderness'.[27] On this evidence we cannot say that it was original for Temple, Shaftesbury or Switzer to praise irregularity at a much later date.

A second reason for hailing Temple as the originator of a new style is his much-quoted praise of Chinese gardens. But Temple had not visited China, or even seen a drawing of a Chinese garden. The new style had almost passed maturity before any Chinese garden ornament apeared in England.[28] It was doubtless important to know that a different style of garden design *was* possible, but in its early stages the new style owed nothing to China. Certainly there was nothing Chinese about Temple's own garden. Shaftesbury does not mention Chinese gardens and Switzer only refers us to Temple on the subject.

The third and most important reason for believing that the three writers contributed to the development of a new style is that they conceived garden design as an art which should imitate nature. Temple wrote that it was not possible to design a good garden 'if nature be not followed' and added that he took this principle 'to be the great rule in this, and perhaps in everything else'.[29] Similarly Shaftesbury stated that 'I shall no longer resist the passion growing in me for

Chiswick House, London, above, and Mereworth Castle, Kent, below, seen in their 'irregular' landscape settings. Both are closely based on Andrea Palladio's design of 1552 for the Villa Capra at Vicenza.

A Palladian villa in a wild setting combines the unexpected detail of the visible world with the concept of perfection, symbolised by the use of the square and the circle in the house plans.

Chiswick House photograph courtesy Michael Lancaster.

things of a natural kind',[30] and Switzer that 'a design must submit to nature'.[31] The three authors were thus united in their praise for nature, and the importance of their remarks turns on the connection between garden design and the axiom that 'art should imitate nature'. Had the meaning of the word 'nature' been fixed there would have been little significance in the connection. But because the late seventeenth and early eighteenth centuries were a time of ferment in philosophy and the sciences, the meaning of the word 'nature' was itself in a state of flux.

The importance of the precise meaning which is attached to the word 'nature' can be shown by considering two alternatives. If nature is used to mean 'essence', as in 'the nature of the case', then the axiom exhorts designers to base their proposals on the essential geometrical forms — the circle, the square, and the rectangle. But if the word is used with the connotation 'unaffected by man', as in 'the world of nature' or 'the natural environment', then the axiom exhorts designers to produce irregular and non-geometrical designs. Between 1700 and 1800 different conceptions of nature were slotted into the axiom that gardens should imitate nature. They generated new styles of garden design but the different conceptions of nature did not replace one another in the English language. A wide range of uses of the word 'nature' remained current, and the various meanings were as confusing in the eighteenth century as they are today. In order to explain how they affected the course of garden design something more must be said about seventeenth century aesthetics and the idea that art should imitate nature.

Seventeenth century aesthetics

Seventeenth century aesthetic theory is variously described by art historians and philosophers as 'rationalist', 'neo-classical' and 'Neoplatonic', but each of these words has also been given more specific meanings. For example 'rationalist' is used as a contrast to 'romantic', 'neo-classical' to describe the period 1750-1850, and 'Neoplatonic' to describe the ideas of the third century philosopher Plotinus. In this book 'rationalist' will be used to describe a theory of knowledge which contrasts with empiricism, and 'Neoplatonic' to mean derived from the writings of Plato. Plato has, of course, been very freely interpreted by later philosophers but the aspect of his aesthetic theory which concerns us has its origins in the Theory of Forms.

This theory rests on the difference between particulars and universals. Particulars are the individual things which compose the visible world. Some are animal, some vegetable and some mineral, but all are imperfect and subject to change. Universals, on the other hand, are general concepts such as straightness, yellowness, beauty and justice. They are perfect and not subject to change. Let us take straightness as an example. It refers to a line which is absolutely and perfectly straight, though we can never see such a line. Every particular example of a straight line will deviate from the universal idea of 'straightness' because of imperfections in the drawing instrument and the surface upon which the line is drawn. We know that nothing could happen to change the concept of straightness, but every example of a straight line can be corrupted. Plato reasoned that since the visible world is composed only of particulars, and since we know that there are such things as universals, another world must exist which is composed only of universals. He called universals 'forms' or 'ideas' and his theory about their

The central portal of the west facade of Notre-Dame, Paris, is arranged in a Platonic hierarchy, showing how the body of Christian knowledge was imitated in the fabric of the cathedral, with everything in its place.

nature and existence is known as the Theory of Forms.

Because the world of forms is perfect and changeless Plato thought it superior to the visible world. He believed that the more we know about forms the better equipped we will be to conduct our lives and the government of our society. From this point of view some forms, such as beauty, truth and justice, are more important than other forms, such as straightness and yellowness. The forms can therefore be arranged in a hierarchy with the most important at the top and the least important at the bottom. In Plato's view the most general and most important form is goodness, which he called the Form (or Idea) of the Good.

Among philosophers there are numerous and ancient disputes concerning Plato's theories. There is some doubt as to whether or not he actually believed in the separate existence of the world of forms, and it may be that the Theory of Forms was only intended as a simile, for Plato loved similes and used many of them. From our point of view what matters is not so much what Plato believed but the manner in which he has been interpreted by artists and aestheticians. It is for this reason that the influence of his ideas is best described as Neoplatonism.

A.N. Whitehead remarked that 'the safest general characterisation of the European philosophical tradition is that it consists in a series of footnotes to Plato'.[32] The discussion of *mimesis* (imitation) in *The Republic, The Timaeus* and *The Laws* was taken up by Aristotle and countless later philosophers. They have argued that since the world of forms is better than the everyday world, artists should imitate the ideal forms in their work. 'Art', we are told by Neoplatonism, 'should imitate nature'. By 'nature' the Neoplatonists meant the world of forms — not the visible everyday world. In the course of its long history the consequences of this axiom have varied according to the different interpretations which have been placed upon 'imitation' and 'nature'. Before discussing the influence of the axiom on garden design it is worth considering some of its effects on the other arts.

The idea that art should imitate nature was transmitted to medieval art by

The Medici Villa at Careggi, where Lorenzo de Medici (the Magnificent) founded his Platonic Academy and reintroduced Plato's works to European culture. The design of the garden has changed since the mid-fifteenth century.

Aristotle. He adopted the idea that art should imitate the forms but did not believe that these existed in a transcendent world. Aristotle's theories had a profound influence on Christian art. Erwin Panofsky has explained how 'the High Gothic cathedral sought to embody the whole of Christian knowledge, theological, moral, natural, and historical, with everything in its place' and was arranged to manifest the 'uniform division and subdivision of the whole structure',[33] and the separate identity of each part. Nature was understood as a Christian version of the hierarchy of forms, as 'the whole of Christian knowledge... with everything in its place'. Imitation was interpreted as the process of manifesting this body of knowledge in the fabric of the cathedral. Thus the central portal of the west facade of Notre-Dame in Paris was arranged visually and structurally to show the hierarchical relationship between the Damned, the Resurrected, the Apostles, the twelve Virtues, the Saints and the Wise and Foolish Virgins.

Although Aristotle's influence displaced that of Plato during the Middle Ages, Plato's works were rediscovered in Renaissance Italy.[34] In 1439 Lorenzo de Medici founded a Platonic Academy in his garden at Careggi outside Florence, and from this point onwards Plato had a direct influence on Renaissance art. Humanist architects, such as Alberti and Palladio (1518-80), studied classical architecture in the light of Plato's theories and rediscovered the fact that Greek and Roman architecture were based on mathematical proportions. Thus the relationship between the width of a column and its height was found to be based on Plato's conception of harmonic proportion and was taken to be an example of architecture imitating the forms. Wittkower has described the manner in which Palladio was inspired by Neoplatonism.[35] His architecture was based on the circle, the square and the principle of harmonic proportion, for Palladio believed them to represent the Forms of the Good, Justice and Harmony. The imitation of these essential forms was a way of producing buildings which partook of the nature of the world.

Similar beliefs underlie the mathematically-calculated 'Cartesian' gardens of the seventeenth century. Descartes did not write on either aesthetics or gardening, but his use of the geometrical method in reasoning led philosophers and artists to seek self-evident axioms on which to base aesthetics. The axiom that art should imitate nature fitted in perfectly with Cartesian philosophy. Nature was understood once again as the essential and universal forms underlying the visible world. We can find the 'geometrical method' in Poussin's use of grids, in Racine's plays, in Le Nôtre's garden designs, and in the formulae which Boyceau gives for calculating the correct relationships between the length, height and width of an avenue. The latter correspond to the formulae which were used by Palladio to work out the mathematical relationship between a pavement and its adjacent arcade.

Neoplatonic ideas also had wide currency in seventeenth and eighteenth century England. We find them in the writings of Dryden, Shaftesbury, Pope, Johnson and Reynolds. In one way or another these authors all tell us that art should

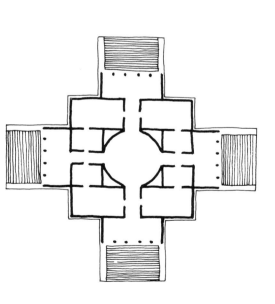

Above, the ground plan of Andrea Palladio's Villa Capra, near Vincenza and, above right, the Villa Capra, built in 1552, as it appears today.

Palladio based his designs on the principle of harmonic proportion, incorporating the circle and the square. The imitation of these 'forms' in architecture was a method by which buildings were enabled to partake of the 'nature' of the world. Photograph courtesy Patrick Goode.

imitate nature. The theory was also taken up by gardening authors and became commonplace. It was expressed by Pope in his famous lines:

> To build, to plant, whatever you intend,
> To rear the Column, or the Arch to bend,
> To swell the Terras, or to sink the Grot;
> In all, let Nature never be forgot.[36]

Pope's garden in Twickenham was essentially an English version of a geometrical French garden. It presents us with another example of the puzzle which was discussed in connection with Temple, Shaftesbury and Switzer. Pope is renowned as one of the prophets of the new English style but his own garden was distinctly French. When Pope writes 'all art consists in the imitation and study of nature',[37] the idea of nature he has in mind is mathematical and Neoplatonic:

> First follow Nature, and your judgement frame
> By her just standard, which is still the same:
> Unerring NATURE, still divinely bright,
> One clear, unchang'd, and universal light, . . .
> Those Rules of old discover'd, not devis'd,
> Are Nature still, but Nature Methodiz'd;
> Nature, like Liberty, is but restrain'd
> By the same Laws which first herself ordain'd.[38]

It is clear that Pope is using 'nature' to refer to the universal forms and the rules of proportion which, in Neoplatonic theory, it is the task of the artist to imitate. However, when Pope writes of 'the amiable Simplicity of unadorned Nature, that spreads over the Mind a more noble sort of Tranquility, and a loftier Sensation of Pleasure, than can be raised from the nicer Scenes of Art',[39] it appears that he is using 'nature' in an entirely different sense: to refer to a natural scene. It is this sense of the word which revolutionised the art of garden design. The use of 'nature' to mean empirical reality was not new but it was given great impetus by the philosophical school known as empiricism. Eighteenth century England saw a steady swing from Cartesian rationalism to the empiricism of Bacon, Hobbes, Locke and Hume. The empiricism which we find in Pope comes directly from the writings of Locke and Shaftesbury.

The influence of empiricism

Empiricism holds that our knowledge of the world comes primarily from experience, and rationalism that it comes primarily from reason. An extreme rationalist would believe that we are born with knowledge of all the universal forms tucked away in our minds, and that we only come to know the world in the light of this knowledge. An extreme empiricist, on the other hand, would believe that our minds contain nothing at birth and only acquire knowledge by seeing and experiencing the world. When applied to aesthetics, rationalism tends towards the view that art should represent the world of the forms, and empiricism to the view that it should represent the world of experience. Rationalist art makes great use of regularity, proportion and mathematics, while empiricist art delights in wildness, irregularity and unexpected details. These two conceptions of art depend on two views of how man comes to know the 'nature' of the world.

John Locke was the most important empiricist philosopher to influence the

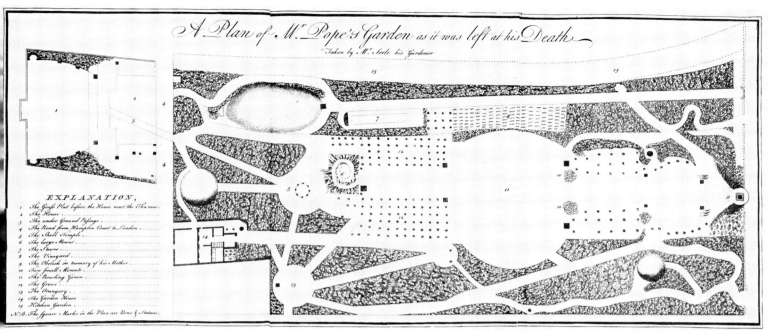

John Serle's plan of Pope's garden. The design is evidently French-inspired, and has always been a problem to those who wish to see Pope as a prophet of the 'English landscape style'.

course of eighteenth century garden design, and it would be fascinating to learn more of his views on gardening. We know that he advised his patron on 'the layout of his gardens', but it was probably on technical matters. His little book on gardening contains nothing on aesthetics but a good deal of information about the cultivation of the vine.[40] Locke's influence on garden design came about through his patron, the first Earl of Shaftesbury, and through his pupil, the third Earl of Shaftesbury.

The third Earl was a firm supporter of the Neoplatonic theory of art. He believed that the artist should represent the simplest and purest forms. 'Why', Shaftesbury asks, 'is the sphere or globe, the cylinder and obelisk preferred; and the irregular figures in respect of these, rejected and despised?' His answer to the question is thoroughly Neoplatonic. Simple and pure shapes are preferred because 'the beautiful, the fair, the comely were never in the matter... but in the form or forming power'.[41] It is clear that Shaftesbury has assigned each of the geometrical shapes a hierarchical position. The sphere and cylinder occupy high positions and the irregular figures lowly positions. Neoplatonists have often interpreted Plato in this manner, but though he does refer to the sphere as 'the most perfect and most like itself of all the figures', Plato himself was uninterested in the position of the other shapes.

It is also notable that Shaftesbury, like Pope, uses the word 'nature' in several different senses. In the following passage he uses 'unnatural' to describe the painter who 'strictly copies life', but 'nature' to describe the scene which he copies: 'A painter, if he has any genius, understands the truth and unity of design; and knows he is even unnatural when he copies nature too close, and strictly copies life'.[42]

The injunction not to copy life too strictly appears to conflict with Shaftesbury's oft-quoted remark that 'I shall no longer resist the passion growing in me for things of natural kind'.[43] The apparent conflict is explained by the presence of a strong current of empiricism running through Shaftesbury's essentially rationalist philosophy. Like Plato, he believed that our knowledge of the forms can be increased by a study of the particulars which compose the visible world. A visual symbol of this idea could be provided by a Palladian villa, based on the circle and square, set in a wild and irregular landscape. Had Shaftesbury lived for another twelve years (i.e. until 1725) he could have seen beautiful illustrations of this idea at Mereworth Castle in Kent, designed by Colen Campbell, and at Chiswick House, designed by Lord Burlington and William Kent (p.19). The small Palladian temples which were later used to adorn Stourhead and many other English landscape gardens also illustrate Shaftesbury's point.

In the middle years of the eighteenth century, when Stourhead was being laid out and Lancelot Brown held the post of Royal Gardener at Hampton Court, there was a balance in the minds of garden designers between the regular and irregular conceptions of nature. By the end of the century the irregular conception had scored a complete victory. William Gilpin's partisan enthusiasm for the rough and rugged aspects of nature turned the Neoplatonic theory of art completely upside down. There is no clearer illustration of what happened than in the writings of William Gilpin's nephew, William Sawrey Gilpin, a nineteenth century landscape gardener.

In 1832 Sawrey Gilpin published *Practical Hints upon Landscape Gardening* in which he expresses his confusion and total exasperation over a footnote in the first edition of Sir Henry Steuart's *Planter's Guide.* Steuart had suggested that if anyone was not so fortunate as to have the use of a Lancelot Brown tree transplanter to produce instant irregularity then, as a temporary expedient, it would be acceptable to plant the trees in circular or oval clumps. Steuart believed that:

> There is no man whose taste has been formed on any correct model, that does not feel and acknowledge the beauty of these elegant forms, the Oval, the Circle, and the Cone . . . and there are few well-educated persons, who will for a moment compare to them a multitude of obtuse and acute angles, great and small, following each other, in fantastical and unmeaning succession.[44]

Sawrey Gilpin was horrified by Steuart's remarks and quoted all the available authorities in an effort to ridicule him. 'Did nature ever bound plantations by a circular or oval form?' he asks and 'are they to be traced in Claude or Poussin — in Wilson or in Turner?'[45] Sawrey Gilpin was also able to invoke the names of William Gilpin, his famous uncle, of Sir Uvedale Price, who had done so much to popularise picturesque irregularity, and of Sir Walter Scott, who had reviewed Steuart's book in *The Quarterly Review.* The really maddening thing for Sawrey Gilpin was that Steuart had claimed, in full accord with Neoplatonism, that the circle and the oval are 'prevalent in all the most beautiful objects in nature'.[46] 'It appears singular', says Gilpin, 'that the evidence on each side of the question before us, should appeal to nature as the foundation of their diametrically opposite systems'.[47] Gilpin recommended 'the author of the *Planter's Guide*' to 'spend a day amidst the splendid scenery of the New Forest'[48] in the hope that the experience would convince him that 'nature' is irregular and not at all like the circles and ovals of a Neoplatonic dream. We do not know if Steuart took Sawrey Gilpin's advice but the footnote on circles and ovals was dropped from later editions of the *Planter's Guide.*

It can be seen from the controversy between Gilpin and Steuart that by the nineteenth century the 'nature' which Gilpin and most landscape gardeners

Sawrey Gilpin hoped the 'splendid scenery' of the New Forest would persuade Steuart that 'nature' is fundamentally irregular.

believed they should imitate was located near the bottom of the Neoplatonic hierarchy of forms. 'Nature' had become the empirical world of everyday experience: not the world of the forms. The steady advance of empiricism, exerting its influence through the axiom that art should imitate nature, became the engine which drove the aesthetic development of garden and landscape design in the eighteenth century. The engine faltered after the turn of the century but flickered back to life towards the end of the nineteenth century in the work of Robinson and Jekyll. Indeed, if abstract art is conceived as an attempt to analyse the nature of the visible world, as will be suggested in Chapter V, then it might be said that a derivative of the engine is chugging away in the garden to this day.

The Italian connection

The progress of garden design towards an empiricist conception of nature was delayed by the overwhelming influence of the Italian countryside. We do not know for certain how the Italian influence arrived in England but we do know why. Designers looked to Italy because of their belief that art should imitate nature, and that nature meant universals or essences. One way of discovering if something was a universal was to check whether it had been accepted by mankind for a long period of time. Poets imitated themes and verse forms from Horace and Virgil. Thinkers went back to the writings of Greek and Roman philosophers. Painters copied antique models: 'Thus the best artists', Shaftsbury tells us, 'are said to have been indefatigable in studying the best statues: as esteeming them a better rule than the perfectest human bodies could afford'.[49] Nothing was more natural than for garden designers to try and discover what the landscape of antiquity had actually looked like.

There were five main ways in which their opinions were formed: by making a grand tour to see Roman remains, like the Temple of Vesta at Tivoli; by purchasing Italian landscape paintings (Shaftesbury is known to have admired Claude); by reading accounts of the villas of the ancients, such as Robert Castell's; by copying the settings of Italian buildings, as was done for the Temple of Four Winds at Castle Howard; and by transposing the techniques of Italian stage design

The Temple of Vesta at Tivoli inspired many tourists to build temples in English gardens.

to garden design.

Which of these five influences was the most important? In my opinion the answer is landscape painting. The objectives of garden design have been traced to Greek and Roman philosophy with the poetry of Virgil and Horace as the most immediate sources. It must have appeared a logical move to look to painting, as poetry's sister art, to discover what the landscape of antiquity actually looked like. Aristotle, whose *Poetics* was the standard seventeenth century text on the imitation of nature, had made a direct comparison of the two arts. Dryden discusses the *Poetics* at length in his preface to DuFresnoy's *The Art of Painting*,[50] and both Claude and Poussin turned instinctively to the Roman poets for themes. Their canvases, illustrating scenes from Virgil and Ovid, filled with remnants of classical architecture and animated by figures in Roman dress, appeared to show a universal ideal of beauty which had been valued since the classical age. At a time when Oxford undergraduates could be fined for challenging the authority of Aristotle, it was natural that designers should look to painting to provide an ideal vision of nature to imitate.

In 1697 Dryden had translated Virgil's works into English and, if we compare an illustration from his translation with an illustration from a contemporary manual on painting (p.31), we can see how closely the visions of antiquity given by poets and painters resemble each other. It is interesting to note that an illustration to Dryden's Virgil was subscribed by 'George London of his Majesties

The Temple of Four Winds at Castle Howard, North Yorkshire, designed by Sir John Vanbrugh in 1726, is one of the most perfect garden temples in England and was inspired by Palladio's Villa Capra (p.23). Writers and painters of the day copied the antique, a practice no less popular among architects and garden designers.

Claude's 'Landscape: Cephalus and Procris Reunited by Diana' illustrates what Sir Kenneth Clark described as 'the most enchanting dream which has ever consoled mankind', and Sir Uvedale Price as 'that mild and equal sunshine of the soul which warms and cheers, but neither inflames nor irritates'.

Paintings such as this became important components of the English landscape ideal. Like much of the thinking of the time, writing and poetry were also inspired by the landscape of antiquity.
Reproduced by courtesy of the Trustees, The National Gallery, London.

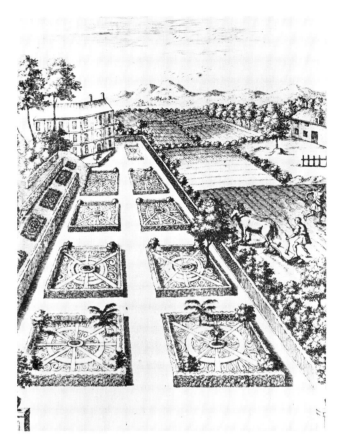

The frontispiece to Timothy Nourse's Campania Felix, *1700, shows a toga-clad happy husbandman ploughing his furrow towards an enclosed seventeenth century garden.*

Royall Garden in St. James's Park'. London became the most famous garden designer of his day.

Claude and Poussin were seen to be illustrating the same rural retirement theme which the poets celebrated. Sir Kenneth Clark has described their paintings as a representation of 'the most enchanting dream which has ever consoled mankind, the myth of a Golden Age in which man lived on the fruits of the earth, peacefully, piously, and with primitive simplicity'.[51] It was an enchanting dream of an 'earthly paradise... a harmony between man and nature'.[52] A seventeenth century gardening author's version of this dream is shown on the frontispiece of Timothy Nourse's *Campania Felix*.[53] Nourse had been a bursar at Oxford but lost his job after being converted to Roman Catholicism. He suffered during the Popish Plot and died in 1699, the same year as Sir William Temple. Like many of their contemporaries, Nourse and Temple came to believe that rural retirement offered the chance of a better life.

We can conclude our discussion of aesthetic theory by saying that when the happy husbandman of Nourse's frontispiece had finished ploughing the field, he reached the representative seventeenth century garden and began its transformation into an eighteenth century English landscape.

The landscape ideal

During the eighteenth century estate owners, no longer content merely to dream of an 'earthly paradise', set about giving reality to the dream. They brought about what has been described as a 'great revolution in taste'.[54] Some authors have tried to single out one factor, such as 'love of nature', 'a revolt against formality', 'romanticism' or 'Chinese influence' as *the* cause of the revolution, but this is misleading. The objective was to make an ideal landscape, and it is not surprising that ideas were collected from many sources to build up the ideal. They came from philosophy, art, politics, economics, horticulture, agriculture, forestry and science; from Greece, Italy, Holland, England, France and China. The grand coalition was then assembled in an English garden.

It appears that the political genius who first brought the coalition together was Addison. Dobrée describes him as 'a very able, very well-read and intelligent populariser of astonishing literary skill' who made known 'the most advanced thought of his time, both philosophically and aesthetically'.[55] Addison's essays of 1712 on the *Pleasures of the Imagination*[56] contain most of the key ideas which went to make up the ideal. The assembly of these ideas is particularly significant: rural retirement, Neoplatonism, Lockian empiricism, landscape painting, and the idea that a country estate can be improved by gardening, forestry and agriculture. None of the ideas was new but several were new bedfellows in 1712. The coalition gained strength from Addison's clear formulation, and the resultant impetus launched garden and landscape design along a path of dynamic change.

An illustration from Dryden's translation of Virgil, 1697. This plate was subscribed by the best known garden designer of the period, George London. If the happy husbandsmen look more wooden than happy it is because they were drawn from antique models instead of from life.

Courtesy The British Library.

An example of a landscape drawing from William Salmon's manual of painting, Polygraphice, *1672. The scene is more like a vision of antiquity than a view of the seventeenth century English countryside. It was probably based on Italian landscape drawings.* Courtesy The British Library.

Petworth, West Sussex, designed by Brown in 1752, has been described by the National Trust as 'one of the supreme achievements of eighteenth century landscape gardening in Europe'.

Many landscape designers who have been influenced by the ideal have given verbal expression to the objectives of their art. The following quotations have been selected from authors who have written in the eighteenth, nineteenth and twentieth centuries. Some of the authors alternate between ideals and practicalities in true Virgilian style. Most of the quotations are concerned only with the making of gardens, but the last two are from designers who have an interest in gardening but whose work extends well beyond the garden boundary.

Stephen Switzer (1682-1745) summarised his philosophy in two lines of 'rustic verse' which he borrowed from Horace's *Ars Poetica*. They are quoted here in the original Latin and in Christopher Hussey's translation:

> *Utile quimiscens, ingentia Rura,*
> *Simplex Munditis ornat, punctum hic tulit omne.*
> (He that the beautiful and useful blends,
> Simplicity with greatness, gains all ends.)[57]

Lancelot Brown (1716-1783) was remiss in not leaving us a full account of his objectives, but a letter has been found by Dorothy Stroud which gives some idea of his opinion on how to make a landscape:

In France they do not exactly comprehend our ideas on Gardening and

Blenheim, Oxfordshire, above, and Petworth, are two of Lancelot 'Capability' Brown's most famous and successful schemes. The gentle 'nature' he sought to imitate was that of the English lowlands with their flowing curves of landscape and river. In both parks the serpentine lakes were made by damming small streams.

Place-making which when rightly understood will supply all the elegance and all the comforts which Mankind wants in the Country and (I will add) if right, be exactly fit for the owner, the Poet and the Painter. To produce these effects there wants a good plan, good execution, a perfect knowledge of the country and the objects in it, whether natural or artificial, and infinite delicacy in the planting &c.[58]

Sir Uvedale Price (1747-1829) was a critic of Lancelot Brown's style, but the following quotation makes it clear that he would not have disagreed with Brown's objectives. It is a most charming statement of the landscape ideal:

The peculiar beauty of the most beautiful of all landscape painters is characterised by *il riposo di Claudio,* and when the mind of man is in the delightful state of repose, of which Claude's pictures are the image — when he feels that mild and equal sunshine of the soul which warms and cheers, but neither inflames nor irritates — his heart seems to dilate with happiness, he is disposed to every act of kindness and benevolence, to love and cherish all around him.[59]

Humphry Repton (1725-1818) was not as confident of his theoretical abilities as of his design skills, and gives rather a conventional description of his professional role: the 'whole art of landscape gardening may properly be defined [as] *the pleasing combination of art and nature adapted to the use of man'*.[60]

Gertrude Jekyll (1843-1932) made few references to the eighteenth century theorists in her writings but the following passage shows how well she understood their importance:

> The free school... teaches us to form and respect large quiet spaces of lawn, unbroken by flower-beds or any encumbrance; it teaches the simple grouping of noble types of hardy vegetation, whether their beauty be that of flower or foliage or general aspect. It insists on the importance of putting the right thing in the right place, a matter which involves both technical knowledge and artistic ability... It teaches us to study the best means of treatment of different sites; to see how to join house to garden and garden to woodland. Repton says most truly: 'all rational improvement of grounds is necessarily founded of a due attention to the character and situation of the place to be improved; the former teaches us what is advisable, and the latter what is possible to be done'.[61]

Patrick Geddes (1854-1930) was a contemporary of Jekyll's and became the first British designer to use the professional title 'landscape architect'.[62] He believed that 'City improvers, like the gardeners from whom they develop, fall into two broadly contrasted schools, which are really, just as in gardening itself, the formal and the naturalistic'.[63] The following quotation from his writings is interesting for its use of the word 'landscape' instead of his own word 'eutopia' to describe the objectives of the planning process:

> Such synoptic vision of Nature, such constructive conservation of its order and beauty... is more than engineering: it is a master-art; vaster than that of street planning, it is landscape making; and thus it meets and combines with city design.[64]

Ian McHarg (b.1920) is a Scots-American landscape architect who shares Geddes' objectives and also makes use of his famous survey-analysis-plan sequence. The first quotation reveals McHarg's Virgilian objectives and the second his Geddesian approach to bringing about a state of harmony between man and nature:

> This book is a personal testament to the power and importance of sun, moon and stars, the changing seasons, seedtime and harvest, clouds, rain and rivers, the oceans and the forests, the creatures and the herbs.[65]...
> Such is the method — a simple sequential examination of the place in order to understand it. This understanding reveals the place as an interacting system, a storehouse and a value system. From this information it is possible to prescribe potential land uses — not as single activities, but as associations of these. It is not a small claim, it is not a small contribution: but it would appear that the ecological method can be employed to... design with nature.[66]

The theme which unites the above quotations from landscape designers can be described as the objective of creating harmony between man and his environment.

The 1976 supplement to *The Oxford English Dictionary* has sanctioned the use of the verb 'to landscape' to describe the process of achieving this objective. It defines 'to landscape' as 'to lay out (a garden etc.) as a landscape; to conceal or embellish (a building, road, etc.) by making it part of a continuous and harmonious landscape'. When used in this way landscape is an evaluative word and should only be applied to a particular kind of place: a place where there is harmony between man and the land. Unfortunately this specialised use of landscape is totally overshadowed by its descriptive use by geologists and geographers to mean 'a tract of land with its distinguishing characteristics and features, especially considered as a product of modifying or shaping processes and agents'.[67]

The earliest use of 'landscape' as a descriptive term is given by the O.E.D. in 1886, when Giekie used it in a book on geology. Hoskins has since popularised its use in this sense with the title of his book *The Making of the English Landscape*.[68]

When landscape is used as a purely descriptive word meaning 'a tract of land' it becomes difficult to comprehend the arts of landscape gardening and landscape design. One wonders how a landscape, or even a garden, can be made without having full control over the sun, wind and rain, and over the movements of men, animals and plants. If, on the other hand, landscape is used as an evaluative word then landscape design becomes comprehensible. It is simply the art of improving places by whatever means are to hand.

The shift in the meaning of landscape between 1650 and 1850 was a consequence of the changes in the use of the word nature between the same dates.

The word landscape was introduced into modern English from the Dutch towards the end of the sixteenth century and at that time was exclusively a painters' term. A landscape was not something which you could walk across, or build, or buy. It was a Platonic form; an ideal place beyond the world of reality and sharing some qualities with paradise itself. Landscape painters hoped to paint a perfect place on canvas after detailed observation and deep reflection on the world as it appeared to their senses. Instructions on how to do this were given by William Salmon in his *Polygraphice,* published in 1672. 'You are to observe the excellences and beauties of the piece but to refuse its vices', he said. And 'by designing each part after that pattern which was perfect [you] might at last present something perfect in the whole'.[69] Salmon also gives a definition of landscape:

> Landskip is that which appeareth in lines the perfect vision of the earth,
> and all things thereupon, placed above the horizon, as towns, villages,
> castles, promontories, mountains, rocks, valleys, ruins, woods, forests,
> chases, trees, houses, and all other buildings, both beautiful and
> ruinous'.[70]

The O.E.D. gives 1598 as the earliest use of landscape as a painters' term, but by 1616 Michael Drayton seems to be anticipating a later use of the word. He describes the river Rothers in the Isle of Oxney as:

> Appearing to the flood, most bravely like a queen,
> Clad (all) from head to foot in gaudy summers green...
> With villages amongst, oft powdered here and there
> And (that the same more like to landskip should appear)
> With lakes and lesser fords to mitigate the heat.[71]

Drayton is using 'landskip' as it if was a design objective and this is exactly what

The Derwent at Chatsworth, Derbyshire, above, was converted by Brown from a tumbling mountain stream into a serpentine river. Repton criticised him for 'checking its noisy course, to produce the glassy surface of a slow moving river'.

By the end of the eighteenth century Repton, and the general public, had come to appreciate the wild scenery of the Lake District, epitomised by Wasdale Head, left. This represents the sublime 'nature' which influenced garden design during the nineteenth century.

it became during the eighteenth century. Addison adopted the usage and remarked in his 1712 essays that 'a man might make a pretty landskip of his own possessions'.[72] Walpole, looking back on sixty years of efforts to do just this, stated in 1771: 'I should choose to call it the art of creating landscape'.[73] He is using the word partly in an evaluative sense and partly in a descriptive sense. The geographical meaning 'a tract of land' is purely descriptive and seems to have arisen out of the belief that landscape should be made to imitate nature. By the end of the nineteenth century 'nature' had ceased to be a Platonic ideal and, since 'landscape' was made to imitate her, she too ended up on the ground as something formed by 'modifying or shaping processes and agents'.

The changes in the use of the words 'nature' and 'landscape' were a key factor in the development of new styles of garden design. At the end of the seventeenth century garden plans were based on the primary geometrical forms, especially the circle and the square, which were believed to occupy the highest positions in the hierarchy of shapes. In the course of the eighteenth century there was a move towards serpentine and then irregular lines, as the concepts of nature and landscape continued their path downwards from the world of the forms. The pattern of evolution is shown in the diagrams on the right (these styles will be described in more detail in Chapters II and III).

During the nineteenth century it was recognised that all these shapes had a place in nature and a style developed which was based on a transition from geometrical shapes in the foreground, through serpentine curves in the middle distance, and outwards to an irregular background, as the diagram below and p.120 show.

The geometrical concept of a Transition Style has had an enormous influence on nineteenth and twentieth century English garden design. It is, however, primarily a plan style and has been overlaid with stylistic details from a variety of sources (as will be described in Chapters IV and V). They include Italian Renaissance gardens, the Arts and Crafts Movement, and modern architecture in the International Style.

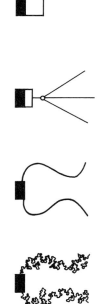

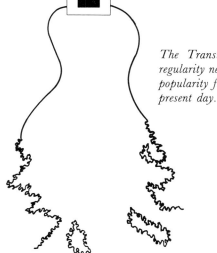

The Transition Style. The idea of forming a transition from regularity near the house to an irregular background has retained its popularity from the closing years of the eighteenth century until the present day.

From top to bottom, the Dutch, Forest, Serpentine and Irregular Styles. The diagrams show the evolution of the geometrical patterns which dominated English garden design in the eighteenth century.

37

The appreciation of Brown

The amazing changes which have taken place in the appreciation of Lancelot 'Capability' Brown as a designer provide a second illustration of the effects which different uses of 'nature' and 'landscape' have had on taste in garden and landscape design. For most of his professional life Brown was hailed as a near-genius and arbiter of taste. His work was seen to be uniquely English and in the most 'natural' style which could be conceived. His status was fully recognised when he was appointed Royal Gardener at Hampton Court in 1764. Three years later the naturalness of his style was praised in an anonymous poem on *The Rise and Progress of the Present Taste in Planting Parks, Pleasure Grounds, Gardens, Etc.* The author gives fulsome praise to Brown and emphasises the naturalness of his schemes:

> He barren tracts with every charm illumes,
> At his command a new Creation blooms;
> Born to grace Nature, and her works complete,
> With all that's beautiful, sublime and great!
> For him each Muse enwreathes the Lawrel Crown,
> And consecrates to Fame immortal Brown.[74]

The conception of nature which the poet had in mind was gentle and pastoral. As David Hume had written in 1748:

> The eye is pleased with the prospect of corn-fields and loaded vineyards, horses grazing, and flocks pasturing: but flies the view of briars and brambles, affording shelter to wolves and serpents'.[75]

Further praise for Brown and his conception of nature came from two important works in 1770. The first was Thomas Whately's *Observations on Modern Gardening,* which Loudon later called 'the grand fundamental standard work on English gardening'.[76] It contains detailed descriptions of several of Brown's designs and practical advice on how to achieve similar effects with ground, woods, water, rocks and buildings. The second, Horace Walpole's essay 'On the History of the Modern Taste in Gardening', was completed in 1770 but not published until 1780. Since its appearance Walpole's essay has exerted an enormous influence over garden historians. Walpole praises Whately's book as 'a system of rules pushed to a great degree of refinement, and collected from the best examples and practice'. After debating a few of the points raised by Whately, Walpole concludes:

> In the meantime how rich, how gay, how picturesque the face of the country! The demolition of walls laying open each improvement, every journey is made through a succession of pictures; and even where taste is wanting in the spot improved, the general view is embellished by variety. If no relapse to barbarism, formality and seclusion is made, what landscapes will dignify every quarter of our island, when the plantations that are making have attained venerable maturity! A specimen of what our gardens will be may be seen at Petworth, where the portion of the park nearest the house has been allotted to the modern style.[77]

The park at Petworth (p.32) had been designed by Brown in 1752 and was often to be painted by J.M.W. Turner in the years to come. Walpole's praise for the

Above, a Brownian scene from The Landscape. *Knight considered it too dull, vapid and smooth. Above right, a Gilpinesque scene from* The Landcape. *Knight loved the broken banks and shaggy mounds.*

design was a way of praising the designer in spite of his resolve to exclude 'living artists' from his essay. It is especially interesting that he praises the 'modern style' for its lack of 'formality and seclusion'. When the reaction against Brown set in the main charges laid against him were his excessive formalism and lack of 'naturalness'. Taste had moved on and the public had come to appreciate 'briars and brambles' and even the wild scenery of the Lake District (p.36). The once-praised 'natural' style of Brown was left beached by the tide of fashion. It now appeared 'artificial', 'stiff' and even 'formal'.

The first serious attack on Brown in this vein came from Sir William Chambers in his *Dissertation on Oriental Gardening,* published in 1772. Chambers criticised 'gardens which differ little from common fields' and praised the Chinese for introducing some of the terrible aspects of nature into their gardens:

> Their scenes of terror are composed of gloomy woods, deep valleys inaccessible to the sun, impending barren rocks, dark caverns, and impetuous cataracts rushing down the mountains from all parts. The trees are ill formed, forced out of their natural directions, and seemingly torn to pieces by the violence of tempests. . .[78]

Chambers made other criticisms of Brown which soon caused his book to be ridiculed, but the substantial criticism contained in the above quotation had been foreshadowed by Walpole and soon became widespread.

The public taste for savage scenery was encouraged by the Reverend William Gilpin. He became 'the high priest of the picturesque',[79] and after the publication of his *Picturesque Tours* began in 1782 he did much to popularise the type of scenery which Chambers liked in Chinese gardens and which Gilpin found in the Wye Valley and the English Lakes. Gilpin published an essay on 'Picturesque Beauty' in 1792 and suggested that the smoothness of a garden was of no use in making a picture and should be roughened with 'rugged oaks instead of flowering shrubs' and by scattering stones and brushwood in the foreground.[80] This line of criticism was directed against Brown's gardens with devastating effect by Price and Knight after 1793.

The first shot came from Knight in his didactic poem *The Landscape:*

> See yon fantastic band,
> With charts, pedometers, and rules in hand,

Advance triumphant, and alike lay waste
The forms of nature, and the works of taste!
T'improve, adorn, and polish, they profess;
But shave the goddess, whom they come to dress;
Level each broken bank and shaggy mound,
And fashion all to one unvaried round;
One even round, that ever gently flows,
Nor forms abrupt, nor broken colours knows;
But, wrapt all o'er in everlasting green,
Makes one dull, vapid, smooth, and tranquil scene...

Hence, hence! thou haggard fiend, however called,
Thin, meagre genius of the bare and bald;
Thy spade and mattock here at length lay down,
And follow to the tomb thy fav'rite Brown:
Thy fav'rite Brown, whose innovating hand
First dealt thy curses o'er this fertile land;
First taught the walk in formal spires to move,
And from their haunts the secret Dryads drove.[81]

Brown's contemporaries would have been most puzzled to see their favourite lampooned for destroying nature and making formal walks and canals. But Knight's criticisms were supported by Uvedale Price and echoed by a host of critics for more than a century. Price was especially critical of Brown's handling of water. He wrote that 'Mr Brown grossly mistook his talent, for among all his tame productions, his pieces of made water are perhaps the most so'.[82] In Price's judgement the serpentine curves of Brown's lakes, and the lack of vegetation on their banks, made them look too like canals:

> In Mr Brown's naked canals nothing detains the eye a moment, and the two sharp extremities appear to cut into each other. If a near approach to mathematical exactness was a merit instead of a defect, the sweeps of Mr Brown's water would be admirable.[83]

Even Repton, who normally supported Brown, thought he had erred in taming the River Derwent (p.36):

> Where a rattling, turbulent mountain-stream passes through a rocky valley, like the Derwent at Chatsworth, perhaps Mr. Brown was wrong in checking its noisy course, to produce the glassy surface of a slow moving river.[84]

In the first phase of his professional career J.C. Loudon admired Gilpin, Price and Knight, and surpassed them in advocating the creation of wild and irregular gardens. He therefore included a vicious attack on Brown in his 1802 *Observations...on...Landscape Gardening*:

> What first brought him into reputation was a large sheet of water which he made at Stowe, in which, as in all his other works, he displayed the most wretched and Chinese-like taste. Wherever his levelling hand has appeared, adieu to every natural beauty! see every thing give way to one

uniform system of smoothing, levelling and clumping of the most tiresome monotony, joined to the most disgusting formality.[85]

The comments from W. Gilpin's nephew, which have already been noted (p.26), were echoed by many nineteenth century authors — who often coupled abuse of his aesthetic taste with remarks on his humble social origins and lack of education. Sir Walter Scott criticised both Kent and Brown. He wrote that their imitations of nature had 'no more resemblance to that nature which we desire to see imitated, than the rouge of an antiquated coquette, bearing all the marks of a sedulous toilette, bears to the artless blush of a cottage girl'.[86]

Criticism of Brown continued in the opening decades of the twentieth century. T.H. Mawson remarked in 1901 that 'had Brown and his followers been content to imitate nature, they would simply have perpetrated so many absurd and expensive frauds, but this imitation did not meet the whole of their misguided practice'.[87]

Even the wise and generous Gertrude Jekyll had a special dislike for Brown:

> The long avenues, now just grown to maturity in many of England's greatest parks, fell before Brown's relentless axe, for straight lines were abhorrent to the new 'landscape' school. Everything was to be 'natural' — sham natural generally, and especially there was to be water everywhere... Possibly his avowed dislike of stonework arose from his incapacity of designing it; certainly when he did attempt anything architectural...his ignorance and want of taste were clearly betrayed.[88]

The Studio was also highly critical of Brown in 1907:

> As he knew practically nothing of his subject, and as, moreover, he prided himself on knowing nothing, he adopted a set formula which expressed his conception of nature, and to this formula he almost always adhered...
> That such narrow conventionality should ever have been accepted as in accordance with the spirit of nature seems to us now almost incredible, and it is difficult to understand how anyone of intelligence could have believed that this sort of empty formality was worthy to be described as landscape gardening.[89]

The revival of Brown's popularity appears to date from the time when a foreign commentator, Marie-Louise Gothein, recognised his work as a distinct style rather than a bad attempt to imitate wild nature. She observed in 1913 that 'Brown was the original advocate of Hogarth's line of beauty'.[90]

The point was taken up by Christopher Hussey seventeen years later in his seminal book, *The Picturesque*. Hussey observed that Brown attempted 'to create landscapes that should arouse emotions, by means of the recipes for beauty evolved by Hogarth and Burke'.[91] He supported his observation with a lovely quotation from Burke which appears to describe a Brown park:

> Most people have observed the sort of sense they have had of being swiftly drawn in an easy coach on a smooth turf, with gradual ascents and declivities. This will give a better idea of the Beautiful than almost anything else.[92]

In 1950, when writing an introduction to Dorothy Stroud's monograph on Brown, Hussey went further and spoke of Brown as 'the most celebrated English

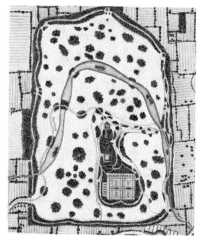

A caricature of a Brownian plan from J.C. Loudon's Country Residences, *1806. Loudon described Brown's design philosophy as 'one uniform system of smoothing, levelling and clumping of the most tiresome monotony joined to the most disgusting formality'.*

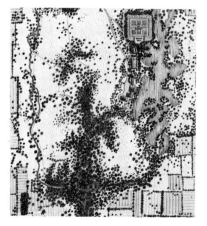

A wild and irregular design by J.C. Loudon from Country Residences, *1806. His design embodies the concept of nature which led to the unpopularity of Brown's style.*

Brown designed both the house and park at Claremont, Surrey, and his supporters have regarded this, and other architectural works, as adequate proof of his ability to handle architectural details. His revival today, as one of the greatest English garden designers, is based on his very distinct style: sweeping lawns, serpentine lakes and carefully placed clumps of trees.

landscape architect of the eighteenth century'.[93] The association of Brown with Hogarth, Burke and Englishness proved irresistible to later critics.

The final seal of approval came from Pevsner in an edition of his *Outline of European Architecture* which makes no reference to Repton, Loudon or Lutyens:

> The great name in the history of mid-eighteenth century gardening is Lancelot Brown (Capability Brown, 1715-83). His are the wide, softly sweeping lawns, the artfully scattered clumps of trees, and the serpentine lakes which revolutionised garden art all over Europe and America.[94]

Hoskins also praised Brown and remarks that:

> In 1764 he created at Blenheim the most magnificent private lake in the country by damming the little river Glyme: 'there is nothing finer in Europe', says Sacheverell Sitwell. He manipulated square miles of landscape in the park, planting trees on a scale consonant with the massive Vanbrugh house.[95]

Nan Fairbrother even defends his clumps: 'This was how Capability Brown established the superb trees in his landscape parks, by planting a close group of saplings and protective shrubs and thinning them as they grew'.[96] In recent years Brown has only been criticised by those writers who continued to lament the loss of the old formal gardens which were destroyed in order to make way for Brownian parks. It is more a criticism of the garden owners than of the designer they employed.[97]

The astonishing change in the appreciation of Brown as a landscape designer is a consequence of the development of garden history as a serious subject. It became evident that he was a stylist, and that the nature which he sought to imitate was not the wild nature of briars, brambles and the Lake District. His love was for that gentler nature which characterises the English lowlands; for serpentine and smoothly flowing curves (pp.32, 33, 36). Serpentine curves can be conceived to occupy an intermediate position in the Neoplatonic hierarchy. They are not as perfect as the circle and square but they have more generality than the random patterns and jagged lines which characterise wild forests and mountains.

Styles of garden design

It is convenient to have names for styles when discussing the history of garden design. The names not only act as *aides-mémoire,* but also focus attention on the changing uses and changing concepts of beauty which have marked the course of garden history. Unfortunately several of the names in general use are not sufficiently limited in scope to be useful for the purpose: 'natural style' and 'landscape style' are typical examples. They are applied indiscriminately to eighteenth century English gardens, but both terms are vague and confusing. Almost any style could be called 'natural'. It depends on one's concept of nature. And which style should be called the 'landscape style'? There are many contenders. Timothy Nourse, whose ideal garden was a walled enclosure, first

Above, Brown's lake at Blenheim, Oxfordshire, has been described as 'the most magnificent private lake in the country'. Above right, a circular Brownian clump at Petworth, in West Sussex, with the protective saplings and shrubs removed.

used the word in connection with gardens in 1699: 'Let there be planted walks of trees to adorn the landskip'.[98]

Addison, in 1712, was the first to speak of *making* a landscape, but Shenstone, in 1754, is usually given the credit for inventing the term 'landscape gardener'. Lancelot Brown is the most famous 'landscape gardener' but in fact he called himself a 'place-maker' (c.1760). His successor, Humphry Repton, was the first professional designer to call himself a landscape gardener (c.1794) but often used 'improver' as an alternative title. The style of his sometime friends Price and Knight was, of any in the eighteenth century, the one most deliberately based on the principles of landscape painting. However, it was the nineteenth century which saw the heyday of 'landscape gardener' as a trade and professional title. Since one or other of the above considerations could be used to justify naming almost any style *the* 'landscape style', it seems best to avoid the term in connection with styles.

The names 'natural style ' and 'landscape style' also tend to encourage the idea that there are only two styles of garden design 'which are really . . . the formal and the naturalistic'.[99] This statement does make the point that lines can be either curvilinear or rectilinear but it obscures the fact that, within these concepts, there exist many different styles of garden design. The styles depend on three main variables: the plan, the hard details and the soft details.

In large gardens and estates the plan is usually the most characteristic feature and over half the styles described in this book take their name from a feature of the plan. In small gardens there is less scope to vary the plan and their appearance tends to be dominated by the design of the hard details (steps, pavings, walls, etc.) and the soft details (herbs, shrubs, trees, etc). The hard and soft details often provide the richness of colour, texture and materials which are among the chief delights of gardens. But they are not of equal durability. A few years neglect can easily destroy a planting design, but walls, steps and fountains often survive when all the other elements of a garden have gone. This is certainly the case with the oldest surviving English gardens.

Eleven main styles of English garden design will be described in the following chapters.

CHAPTER II
1650-1740: The Enclosed, French and Dutch Styles

The fountain in Bushey Park, Richmond, by Francesco Fanelli, was originally sited in an enclosed garden at Somerset House and was one of the most elaborate garden fountains of the seventeenth century.

The Enclosed Style

Gardening has been popular in England at least since Roman times but no complete gardens and few records survive from the period before 1650. Such evidence as we do have about the condition of pre-Civil War gardens comes from books, estate records, travellers' tales, topographical drawings and occasional glimpses in the corners of portrait paintings. There are also a number of garden walls and a few fountains, grottoes, steps and related features which survive from Tudor and early Stuart times.

All the evidence shows that early English gardens were essentially rectangular walled enclosures which provided their owners with somewhere to grow plants and an opportunity to enjoy some of the pleasures of outdoor life. In the Middle Ages a garden of this type was known as a *hortus conclusus* (*L. hortus* a garden or orchard, *conclusus* closed off). Its most important ornaments were flowers, herbs and trellis work. The joys of an enclosed garden were celebrated by Abbot Strabbo in his best-selling poem 'Hortulus':

> Though a life of retreat offers various joys,
> None, I think, will compare with the time one employs
> In the study of herbs, or in striving to gain
> Some practical knowledge of nature's domain
> Get a garden! What kind you may get matters not...
> The advice given here is no copy-book rule
> Picked up second-hand, read in books, learned at school,
> But the fruit of hard labour and personal test
> To which I have sacrificed pleasure and rest.[1]

The history of English garden design after 1500 and before 1650 is covered by Roy Strong in *The Renaissance Garden in England.*[2] It is a history of the stages by which the *hortus conclusus* of the Middle Ages evolved into an English version of the Italian Renaissance garden. The accession of Henry VIII in 1509 marks the point at which gardens became a symbol of the power and prestige of the court. For two centuries after this date the kings and queens of England were leaders of taste in garden design and used their gardens, and those of their nobles, as the settings for parties, masques and other courtly festivities which took place in Italian gardens. Knowledge of Italian gardens first arrived via France, but by 1600 travellers were returning from Italy with personal knowledge of their wonders.

Roy Strong has identified four styles of garden design which flourished in England between 1500 and 1640: the heraldic garden (c.1500-50), the emblematic garden (c.1550-1600), the mannerist garden (c.1600-25) and the eclectic garden (c.1625-40). The physical details and the symbolic significance of these styles are analysed by Strong with great skill but he acknowledges that even the sophisticated mannerist garden 'essentially remains, however, the old *hortus conclusus*. It is a walled enclosure within which nature tamed by art is made to fulfil the wildest of

A restored knot garden at Boscobel, Shropshire. Boscobel is a good example of a modest seventeenth century retreat and the knot garden is seen, as was intended, from an upstairs window.

The mount at Boscobel with its restored summer house — a feature of mid-seventeenth century enclosed gardens from which one could view the surrounding countryside. The oak tree, in which Charles II took refuge in 1651, has died, but the tree in the fenced enclosure is said to have been found growing beside the original tree (p.50).

Bingham's Melcombe, Dorset. The yew hedge dates from the fifteenth century and bounds a hortus conclusus.

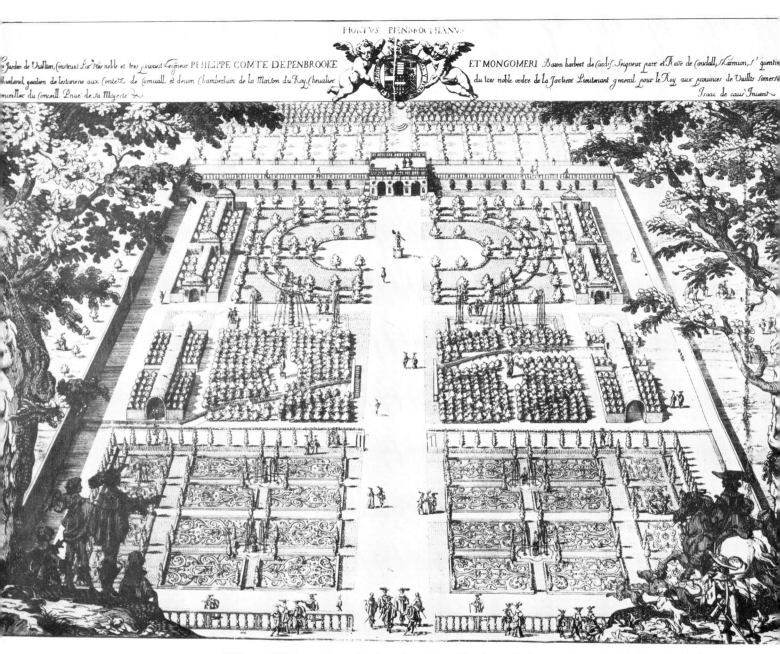

HORTVS PENBROCHIANVS

Le Jardin de Vuilton, Construict Par tres noble et tres puissant Seigneur PHILIPPE COMTE DE PENBROOKE ET MONGOMERI Baron herbert de Cardif. Seigneur parr et Rasse de Candall, Marmion, St quentin dhieland, gardien de lestanerie aux Contez de Cornuall et devon Chamberlain de la Maison du Roy, Chevalier du tres noble ordre de la Jartiere Lieutenant general pour le Roy aux provinces de Vuilts somerset conseiller du Conseill Prive de sa Majeste &c.

Isaac de caus Invent

Wilton, Wiltshire. An enclosed garden designed by Isaac de Caus and completed before the Civil War. It was one of the most famous gardens of its day but the original layout has not survived.

mannerist fantasies, above all by means of the new hydraulics'.[3] It is for this reason that a single diagram (far right) can be used to indicate the style of English gardens at the start of the period covered by this book.

The influence of the Renaissance on English gardens was of great importance but its main impact was on the gardens of the aristocracy, and even here, as Strong notes, it was 'a piecemeal affair' and 'never altogether logical and doctrinaire'.[4] The diagram represents both the aristocratic gardens as well as the large number of less stately gardens which survived in 1650 and bore an even closer resemblance to medieval gardens. Boscobel in Shropshire, where Charles II hid in an oak tree after his defeat in 1651, is a good example of a modest seventeenth century rural retreat (pp. 45 and 50).

From the point of view of the future development of English gardens the most important of the styles identified by Strong was the eclectic garden. It is well represented by Moor Park in Hertfordshire. Sir William Temple, whose influence on the subsequent history of English gardens was discussed in the previous chapter, greatly admired this garden as a young man. He spent his honeymoon there in 1655 and remembered it as 'the sweetest place, I think, that I have ever seen in my life, either before or since, at home or abroad'.[5] His description of Moor Park is one of the best surviving accounts of a garden made in the years preceding the Civil War. The estate was granted to Lucy Harington, Countess of Bedford, by James I and the design of the garden is attributed by Strong to Isaac de Caus.

Moor Park lay on a gentle slope and contained three large rectangular enclosures stepping down a hillside. The first enclosure lay at the top of the slope and in front of the house. It was, Temple's description continues, 'a quarter of all greens. . . adorned with rough rock work and fountains'. Lower down the

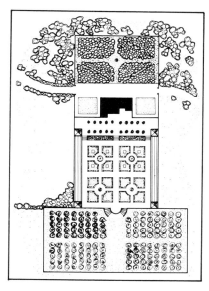

Reconstruction of the plan of the garden at Moor Park, Hertfordshire.

The Enclosed Style: knot gardens, a mount and an orchard are contained within a rectangular enclosure.

'Prospect of the Pierrepont House, Nottingham', British School, c.1708-13. The garden was laid out after 1677, and this illustration, though without the summer houses and cloisters, gives a good impression of the second enclosure at Moor Park, Hertfordshire, as described by Sir William Temple (pp.47 and 49). Courtesy Yale Center for British Art, Paul Mellon Collection.

The water feature at Bramham Park, West Yorkshire, is a clear sign of French influence on English garden design. It was designed by the owner, Robert Benson, and was virtually complete when John Wood drew a plan of the gardens c.1725.

André Mollet, in his Jardin de Plaisir, *1651, recommended the use of straight walks, statues, fountains, waterworks, canals, turf parterres. The book was a vital influence on formal gardens in France, Holland and England.*

slope, and on the other side of the house, lay the next enclosure. It had a terrace adjoining the house and three flights of steps leading down to a very large parterre, which was 'divided into quarters by gravel walks and adorned with two fountains and eight statues'. There were summer houses at each end of the terrace and at the far corners of the parterre. Shady cloisters with stone arches and climbing plants ran along two sides of the parterre and, from the front, two further flights of steps led around an Italianate grotto to a third enclosure. No illustrations of the garden survive but the painting of Pierrepont House in Nottinghamshire gives a good impression of the second enclosure at Moor Park. A seventeenth century terrace of similar character exists at Ham House in London.

The third and lowest enclosure was 'all fruit trees ranged about the several quarters of a wilderness which is very shady'. Something of the character of the third enclosure is shown by the photograph of the walled orchard at Penshurst in Kent (p.50).

Temple speaks wistfully of Moor Park as though it had fallen into neglect by 1685, but since he had 'passed five years without once going to town' it may be that he simply knew nothing of its condition. Many of the royal and courtly gardens which were made in the reign of Charles I did suffer from neglect and deliberate destruction following his execution. During his reign garden design had become associated with the 'Divine Right of Kings', and was seen as 'an assertion of the royal will' — gardens being places in which nature was tamed by art.[6] When the Parliamentarians came to power they despised the Royalist gardens for the social life which they fostered and the principles which they represented. Although a large number of less stately enclosed gardens were still in existence in 1700, few were destined to survive the stylistic revolution of the coming century.

The key/legend visible in the illustration:

1 Boscobel House
2 White Ladies
3 Boscobel garden
4 Part of the Mount in the Garden wherein his Ma.ie sate
5 The back door through which his Ma.ie past to seeke the Oake
6 Boscobel Wood
7 A Stone House in the Wood
8 The Royal Oake in w.ch his Ma.ie and Col. Carlos sate
9 Spring Coppice
10 Six men with their Pendents under a Tree there
11 His Ma.tie shewn marching from White Ladies
12 The Plain between Boscobel Wood and Spring Coppice

Boscobel, Shropshire, in 1660. This is the garden in which the future Charles II hid from Cromwell's troops after the battle of Worcester in 1651 (p. 45). The garden was designed as a retreat in troubled times. Courtesy the British Library.

The walled orchard at Penshurst, Kent, gives us an idea of the lowest enclosure at Moor Park, Hertfordshire, described by Sir William Temple. Temple lived at Penshurst as a boy, after the death of his parents.

50

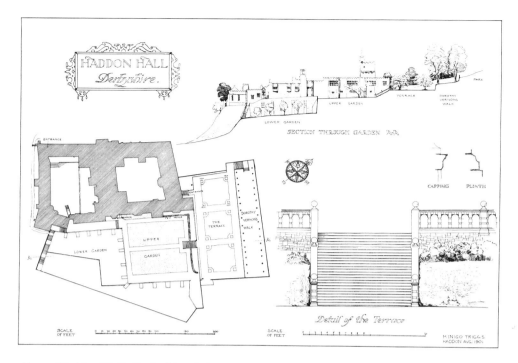

Above, Haddon Hall, Derbyshire. It is a rare example of an enclosed garden which has survived in good condition. Below, St. Osyth's Priory, Essex. The garden layout is recent but the gatehouse dates from c.1475 and the enclosing wall from c.1550.

Honsholredyk (Honselaarsdijk), a famous Dutch garden near The Hague, with a moat round the castle and drainage canals round the perimeter. In France canals were more likely to be decorative garden features, while in Holland the nature of the low-lying land and the need for drainage meant canals were incorporated into garden designs for both practical and aesthetic reasons. (See also pp.63-73.)

Courtesy The British Library.

'The Southeast Prospect of Hampton Court, Herefordshire', by Leonard Knyff (1650-1721), gives an excellent impression of London and Wise's work. Note the 'Dutch' garden characteristics: parterres, a canal, summer houses and half-hearted avenues. (See also pp.65-6.)
Courtesy Yale Center for British Art, Paul Mellon Collection.

Versailles, the most famous garden in France, was designed by André Le Nôtre between 1661 and 1715. The avenues symbolised man's domination of nature and Louis XIV's power over his people.

The French Style

The art of garden design did not flourish under the Commonwealth but revived after the Restoration. For half a century after 1660 royal patronage recovered its pre-Civil War importance, and since the English monarchs had either French or Dutch sympathies they looked across the Channel for much of their inspiration. Charles II had been exiled in France for nine years and admired both the style of the French court and the gardens which Le Nôtre made at Vaux-le-Vicomte (1656-61) and Versailles (1661-1715), while William III, who reigned in England from 1688 to 1702, was a Dutch prince with Dutch tastes. Although it is not easy to determine the relative importance of the two sources of design ideas, there was a distinct tendency for families with Royalist and Catholic sympathies to favour French gardens and for families with Parliamentarian and Protestant sympathies to favour Dutch gardens.

The stylistic differences between France and Holland in the second half of the seventeenth century were largely matters of emphasis. France was a well-wooded and agriculturally-backward country where land was plentiful and the monarch possessed of absolute power. It could afford the space for large hunting forests and avenues leading towards distant horizons. The avenues made it easier to hunt the stag and symbolised both man's domination over nature and the King's dominion

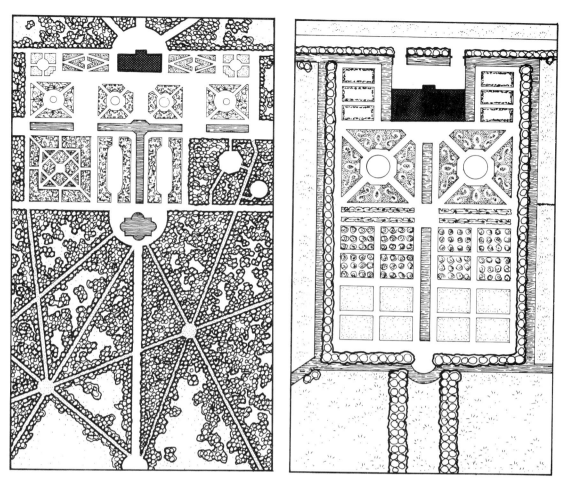

Above, the French Style in France: an elaborate system of parterres and intersecting avenues organised round a central axis. Above right, the Dutch Style in Holland: parterres, canals and orchards in a rectangular enclosure with avenues projecting into farmland.

over his people.

In Holland, on the other hand, there was no desire to proclaim the monarch's absolute power and it was inconceivable that the polder lands, which had been won from the North Sea at great cost, should be used either for hunting forests or for vast unproductive gardens.

The aesthetic ideas which produced Vaux-le-Vicomte and Versailles, when interpreted in Holland with Dutch horticultural expertise, led to an emphasis on immaculate parterres and topiary. Canals, a feature of French gardens, were a necessity in the Dutch lowlands to keep the water table low, though they were often planned as part of a garden and are thought of as characteristically Dutch.

Avenues, valued in Holland for aesthetic reasons, could not be created on a French scale by clearing vistas through ancient hunting forests, and were often no more than lines of newly planted trees extending through agricultural land. The two styles are shown diagramatically above. Both owe a great deal to André Mollet's *Jardin de Plaisir,*[7] which recommended the use of straight walks, statues, fountains, waterworks, canals, turf parterres and *parterres de broderie* (p.49), and was a vital influence on Le Nôtre and on formal gardens in France, Holland and England.

The popularity of the French Style in England undoubtedly received a great

'Greenwich from One Tree Hill', painted c.1680 and attributed to J. Vorstermans. The painting shows The Queen's House and a newly planted avenue of trees in Greenwich Park.
Courtesy of the National Maritime Museum, Greenwich.

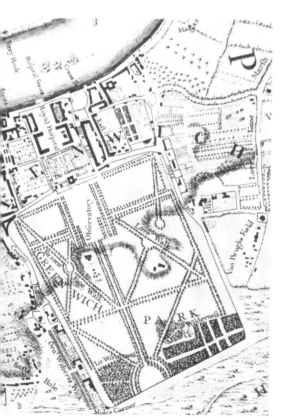

boost from the restoration of Charles II. Charles had spent most of his exile in France and when he returned home he wished to rule as a 'Sun King' and adopt the French style of garden design. Neither ambition was realised to a significant degree. He is thought to have taken advice from Le Nôtre himself on St. James's and Greenwich Parks but even these projects, the best examples of the French Style in England, were pale shadows of their French predecessors. They were small in size and the avenues were formed with single lines of trees.

At Greenwich the visual continuity of the main axis was broken by two sharp changes of gradient along its length and a giant flight of grass steps had to be made to carry the eye up the gradient. John Evelyn, whose *Sylva*[8] gave a great impetus to English forestry, lived near Greenwich and may have advised on the layout. The avenues were made out of lines of trees, like the walks in Evelyn's own garden at Sayes Court, and were enclosed within a boundary wall. Since no forest trees were planted in enclosed gardens, the ancient sweet chestnuts in Greenwich may be the oldest forest trees in any English park or garden.

At St. James's Park a long rectangular canal occupied the centre of the design and The Mall, which is the only feature of the original layout to have survived, was laid out on the north side to provide a space in which to play a type of croquet known as pal-mal, a game which came to England from France. As at Greenwich the avenues were contained within the park boundary.

Rocque's plan of Greenwich Park. Le Nôtre is thought to have advised on the design of both Greenwich and St. James's Park, but he did not visit England, and both parks are pale shadows of his work in France.

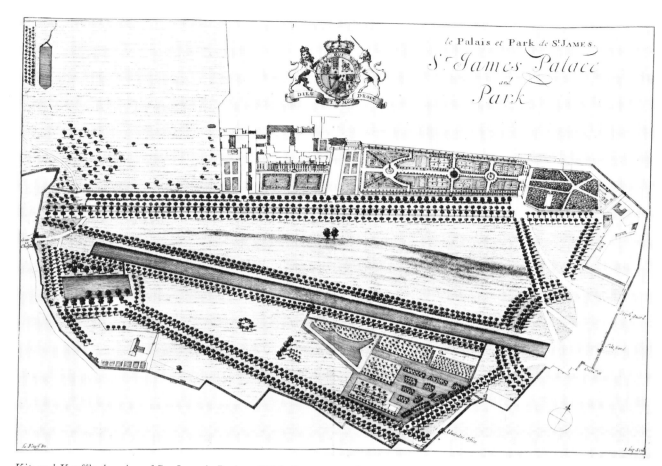

Kip and Knyff's drawing of St. James's Park, c.1700. It was a good example of the French Style in England before it was redesigned in the nineteenth century. Courtesy The British Library.

Levens Hall, Cumbria. The garden was laid out by Guillaume Beaumont, a Frenchman, though the topiary is always considered to be a Dutch feature. Such a combination illustrates the confusion which can be caused by being too specific about French and Dutch influences on English gardens.

An avenue in Greenwich Park which has been made by planting lines of trees on sloping ground.

The sweet chestnuts in Greenwich Park may be the oldest surviving forest trees to have been planted within a garden wall.

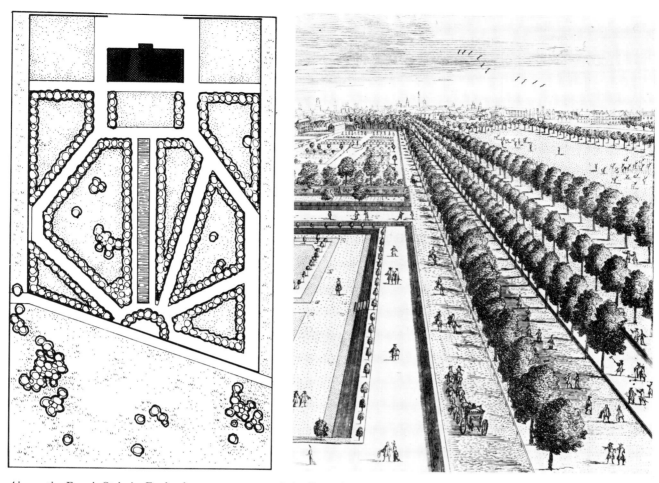

Above, the French Style in England: avenues were made by lines of trees and contained within a boundary wall. Above right, The Mall as illustrated in Stowe's Survey of London. *A game of pal-mal is in progress in the bottom right hand corner.* Courtesy The British Library.

The intended use of Charles II's parks was, however, decidedly French. He wished them to be a focus for court life and St. James's Park, like Versailles, was a place for high society to meet and catch an occasional glimpse of the King:

> The Park was by this time a much-frequented spot, and crowds delighted to watch the King and his courtiers displaying their dexterity [at pal-mal]. Charles II is more intimately connected with St. James's Park than any other great personage. He sauntered about, fed his ducks, played his games, and made love to fair ladies, all with indulgent, friendly crowds watching. He stood in the 'Green Walk' beneath the trees, to talk to Nell Gwynn in her garden 'on a terrace on the top of the wall' overlooking the Park; and shocked John Evelyn, who records in his journal that he heard and saw 'a very familiar discourse between the King and Mrs. Nelly'.[9]

Charles also liked to walk his dogs in the park. St. James's was the heart of London's social life and even in cold foggy weather the most beautiful society ladies were to be seen taking the air in flimsy dresses. This was an English version of the Versailles where Louis XIV's attendants used to go before him to clear a path through the large crowds in his park and a man had only to wear a sword to gain admittance. Greenwich Park was a country estate in the seventeenth century but it was a popular place to visit. Samuel Pepys often went there and recorded in his diary a pleasant afternoon in 1662 when he went 'with all the

Ham House, Richmond. The avenue outside the enclosed garden was not shown on the plan of 1610, but does appear on a plan dated 1671. This addition is significant, for the projection of trees outwards into the countryside signposts the future development of English garden design.
Courtesy Michael Lancaster.

children by water to Greenwich, where I showed them the King's yacht, the house, and the park, all very pleasant'.[10] He later went with Lady Carteret who walked up the hill and down again with a page carrying her train.

Three members of the Mollet family are known to have worked on St. James's Park in the 1660s and to have trained John Rose who became keeper of the park when the Mollets left England. Rose was the first in a long succession of gardeners to the King and aristocracy. They worked either for or with each other and dominated English garden design for at least a century after the Restoration. John Rose (1621-77) employed George London (d.1714) and Henry Wise (1653-1738). London and Wise went into partnership and later employed Stephen Switzer (1682-1745) and Charles Bridgeman (d.1738). After London's death Wise took Bridgeman into partnership.[11] Bridgeman later worked with William Kent (1685-1748), and Kent with Lancelot Brown (1716-83).

The men who stand at the beginning and end of the chain had famously different tastes. Rose admired Le Nôtre, Versailles and French gardens. Brown was the creator of Blenheim and a uniquely English 'parkland' type of landscape. The evolutionary process by which Brown's style developed from the French Style is of great historical interest. Unfortunately the paucity of records makes it very difficult to sort out who did what and in which style. It appears that the five designers who worked after Rose and before Brown responded to more than one stylistic influence. If the styles are given names, and a degree of simplification is

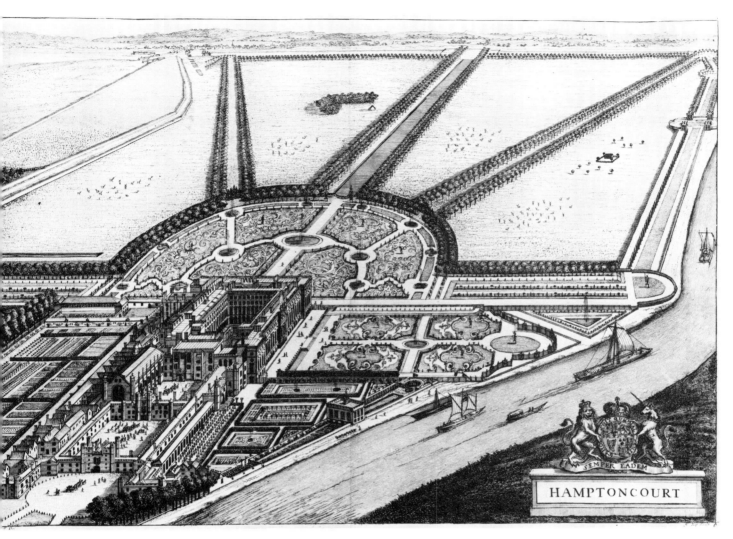

Kip and Knyff's drawing of Hampton Court, c.1700, shows the goose-foot avenues which may have been designed by London and Wise. The semi-circular parterre no longer exists, but deserves to be restored.
Courtesy The British Library.

A chestnut avenue in Bushey Park, Richmond-upon-Thames, designed by the royal gardeners London and Wise.

The avenues at Hampton Court are still composed of single lines of trees. By the end of the seventeenth century so many of England's forests had been cleared that there were few parks where avenues could be made by cutting through existing woodland.

Avenue in Kensington Gardens, designed by Wise and Bridgeman. Their avenues were intended to be used for courtly recreation. This one is seen on a summer Sunday.

A forest avenue at Tynningham, East Lothian.

accepted, then the evolutionary process can be shown in tabular form:

Style	Main exponents	Lesser exponents
French	The Mollets and Rose	London and Wise
Dutch	London and Wise	Switzer and Bridgeman
Forest	Switzer and Bridgeman	Kent
Serpentine 1*	Kent and Bridgeman	Switzer
Serpentine 2*	Brown	Kent

* The two phases of the Serpentine Style are described in Chapter III as the Augustan and the Brownian.

London and Wise certainly admired French gardens. They published a modified translation of a French gardening book[12] and London met Le Nôtre when sent to France by Rose in 1698. Some aspects of their work is distinctly French: it is probable that London and Wise laid out the radiating goose-foot avenues at Hampton Court, Richmond-upon-Thames, and certain that they designed the adjoining chestnut avenues in Bushey Park. These avenues (p.61) were made by planting single lines of trees in the Dutch manner but the radial pattern originates from France. It was fully developed at Badminton in Gloucestershire. The avenues which radiate from the Round Pond in Kensington Gardens, London, were planned by Wise and Bridgeman between 1726 and 1728. Wise took Bridgeman into partnership in 1726. It seems likely that the senior partner was responsible for the design and the junior partner for its execution.

The Dutch Style

The Dutch Style in England was characterised by an emphasis on parterres, topiary, water features, orchards and the planting of avenues in the countryside (see diagram right and p.52). Little survives of London and Wise's executed work but sufficient drawings exist to give an impression of their design practice, which was more Dutch than French. Switzer

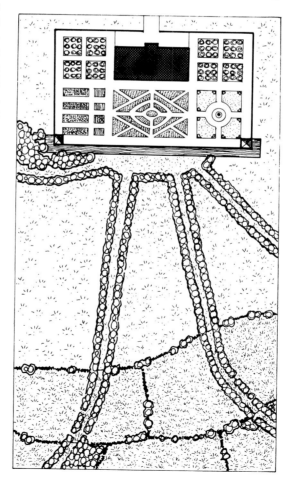

The Dutch Style in England: an enclosed garden with parterres, a canal and an orchard, with avenues outside the wall.

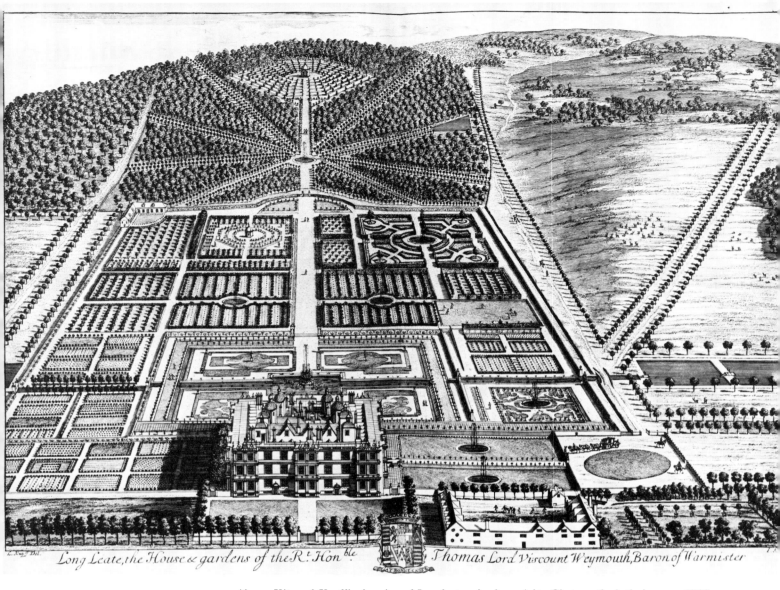

L. Knyff Del.   Long Leate, the House & gardens of the R.t Hon.ble   Thomas Lord Viscount Weymouth, Baron of Warmister

Above, Kip and Knyff's drawing of Longleat and, above right, Chatsworth, both drawn c.1700. Longleat and Chatsworth were George London's most important garden designs and are more Dutch than French in style.   Courtesy The British Library.

described London as superintendent of their majesties' gardens and director-general of most of the gardens and plantations of Great Britain,[13] but in fact he and Wise were great designers of parterres and only occasional designers of avenues and plantations. The parterres were simple by French standards. They had water features, statues and topiary but little embroidery or scroll-work. The avenues were occasionally formed by cutting through existing woods but more often by planting lines of trees. London's most important commissions were the gardens at Longleat and Chatsworth. Both were dominated by extensive parterres and had lines of trees projecting into farmland. At Longleat there was also a small star of avenues which occupied a smaller area than the parterre and could not be compared to a French hunting forest.

The best surviving example of London and Wise's work is at Melbourne Hall in Derbyshire (pp. 66 and 67). The garden was made between 1696 and 1705 by Thomas Coke who also had a hand in its design. A large part of the site is given over to a parterre, while another extensive area is occupied by a grove of irregularly planned avenues which display a taste for axial vistas but not the will

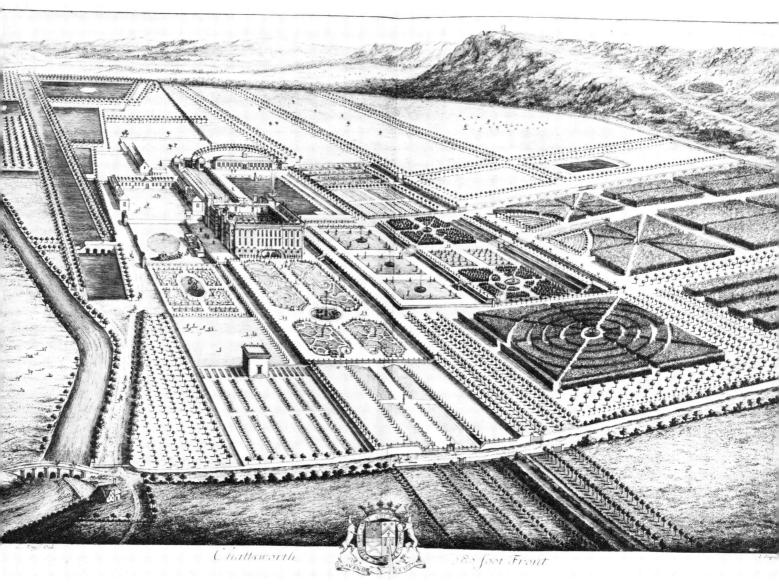

Chatsworth · 280 foot Front

to align them with the main axis of the house and garden. As at Longleat the grove appears to be an addition to the layout rather than its main feature. The parterre has now became a lawn and is marred by a variety of specimen trees which have replaced London and Wise's topiary.

Henry Wise worked at Blenheim with Vanburgh. The division of work between the garden designer and the architect is not known but it is likely that Wise designed the large parterre behind the house, which has gone, and the single avenue in front of the house which survives and is being replanted where necessary. In Kensington Gardens Wise designed a series of parterres and a mount which have been replaced by a modern 'Dutch' garden. There is another modern 'Dutch' garden at Hampton Court in Richmond-upon-Thames (p.67), but the large semi-circular parterre which Wise certainly maintained, and may have designed (p.61), has been replaced by a grotesque semicircle of yew trees. It is also probable that Wise designed the famous maze at Hampton Court. He became a rich man and retired to a country house with a parterre and avenue garden at Warwick Priory. The earthworks for the garden survive in a public park, but the Priory building was moved to America in the 1920s and the County Records Office has been built on the site.[14]

The painting of 'The Southeast Prospect of Hampton Court in Herefordshire' by Knyff (p.53) gives a better impression of London and Wise's work than any surviving garden. The design has been attributed to London and is essentially

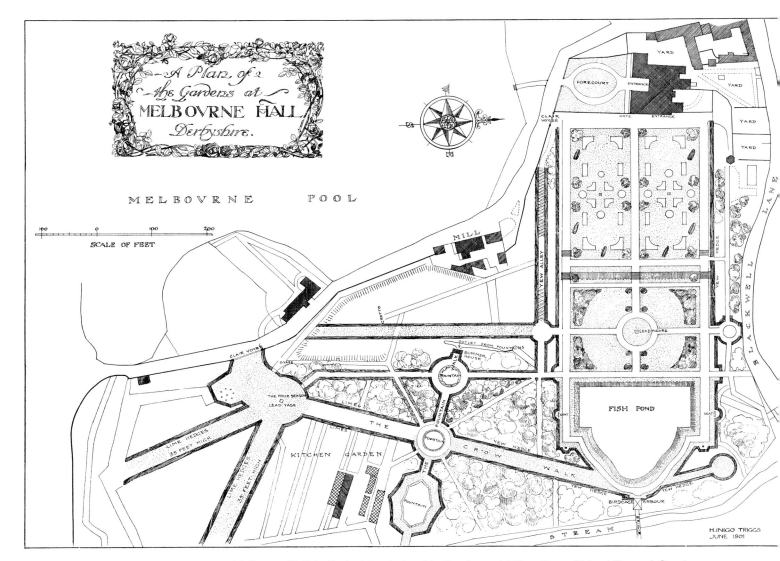

Melbourne Hall in Derbyshire, designed by London and Wise. From Triggs' Formal Gardens.

Dutch. Parterres flank the house on all sides and a canal with two summer houses runs across the front of the garden. Although the avenues radiate from the house, they are clearly an afterthought; they have been made with lines of trees running through agricultural land and appear to lose all sense of purpose on reaching the hills. The painting has a distinct resemblance to the drawing of Sir William Temple's own garden at Moor Park in Surrey, which might have been drawn by Kip or Knyff.[15] Temple's estate was designed c.1680 and named in remembrance of Lucy Harington's Moor Park in Hertfordshire where Sir William and his wife Dorothy had spent their honeymoon in 1655 (pp. 47 and 49). The description of Moor Park in Surrey in Temple's essay *'Upon the Gardens of Epicurus'*[16] is the best written account of a garden in the Dutch style. Temple was a Protestant who admired the Dutch but hated the French 'upon account of their imperiousness and arrogance to foreigners'.[17]

The illustration of Moor Park, Surrey (p.68), shows six large enclosures and numerous sub-divisions. One of the enclosures is laid to grass and was probably used for bowling. Three of the other main enclosures are laid out as knots and parterres and the remainder are used for growing fruit and vegetables. Some topiary can be seen, which takes the form of small pyramids and cubes of the kind

66

The grove at Melbourne is clearly part of the garden, and was not intended to be a hunting forest. The pool in the foreground of this c.1910 photograph is in the Fountain Walk in the plan opposite.

The modern 'Dutch' garden at Hampton Court in Richmond.
Courtesy Michael Lancaster.

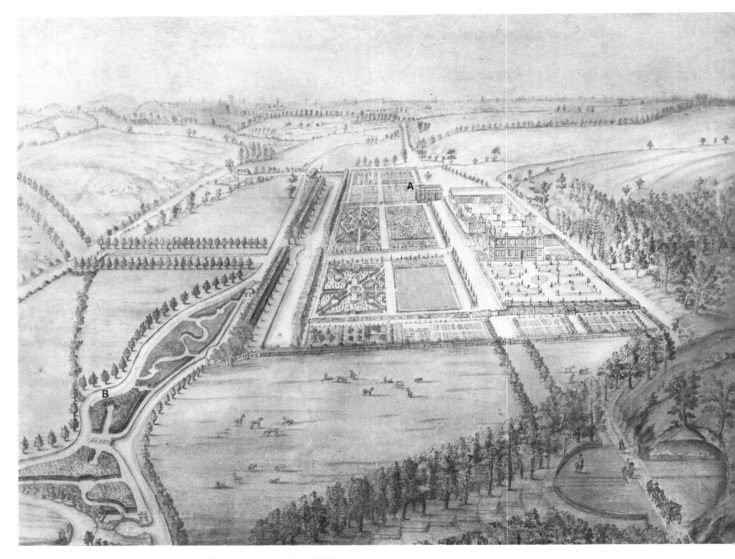

Moor Park in Surrey, Sir William Temple's garden. It is Dutch in style and resembles Hampton Court in Herefordshire (p.53). Note the serpentine stream in the bottom left corner — one of the earliest irregular features on an English garden plan. The letters A and B refer to the next two illustrations. Courtesy Surrey County Library.

which were later ridiculed by Pope, who was a Catholic with French sympathies. The pleached lime walk and the canal at the bottom of the garden are typically Dutch. On the left of the drawing a serpentine stream can be seen wriggling in its efforts to enter the garden. Hussey has suggested that the presence of this line corresponds to Temple's famous remarks on the desirability of irregularity in gardens.[18]

One of the main pleasures of Temple's garden was the dry gravel paths which were so much more convenient to walk on than the muddy unpaved public roads and country paths. The ladies of the house could take the sun and air, safe from wild animals and brigands. After the pleasure of watching the plants grow came

Opposite above, the banqueting house and the remains of the enclosed garden at Moor Park, Surrey. The area is marked A on the illustration above. Opposite, the serpentine section of the river at Moor Park, Surrey. It is marked B on the illustration above.

The restored garden at Penshurst, Kent, gives an impression of Sir William Temple's parterres at Moor Park, Surrey.

Heere I have made the true Lovers Knott
To ty it in Mariage was never my Lott.
This Scale will serve for 3. other Knots folowing.

Above, a design for a knot garden, from Blake's The Compleat Gardener's Practice, *1664, which would have been fairly simple to execute. Right, an elaborate design for a large* parterre de broderie *by Le Blond.* Courtesy The British Library.

A large Parterre of Compartiments.

A modern reconstruction of 'the true Lovers Knott' at Barnsley House in Gloucestershire.

the profit of harvesting fruit and vegetables for the kitchen.

In his essay, 'Upon the Gardens of Epicurus', Temple took a Virgilian interest in fruit but says little about flowers and explains his omission as follows:

> I will not enter upon any account of flowers, having only pleased myself with seeing or smelling them, and not troubling myself with their care, which is more the ladies' part than the men's.

Bacon's jest of 1625 that 'As for the making of knots or figures with divers coloured earth, that they may be under the windows of the house on that side which the garden stands, they be but toys; you may see as good sights many times in tarts',[19] also made the point that the ladies were responsible for domestic activities — in this case making the knot garden and cooking the tarts. Indeed, the patterns for knot gardens were sometimes provided by the same tradesmen who supplied embroidery patterns.[20]

The contemporary books which dealt with flowers were known as herbals, and presumably belonged in the ladies' parlour rather than the gentlemen's study. Herbs were essential for cooking and medical care, and knowledge of them was a necessary part of a woman's education. John Parkinson,[21] the author of the most popular seventeenth century herbal, was an apothecary but gave more attention to flowers than his predecessor John Gerard.[22] Parkinson also illustrated some patterns for knot gardens which, in fact, do resemble embroidery patterns.

The patterns which can be seen in Temple's garden are of intermediate complexity between the traditional knot garden and the elaborate *parterre de broderie* as developed by Claude Mollet, Jacques Boyceau and Le Blond. Temple does not say what flowers were planted at Moor Park but many other contemporary

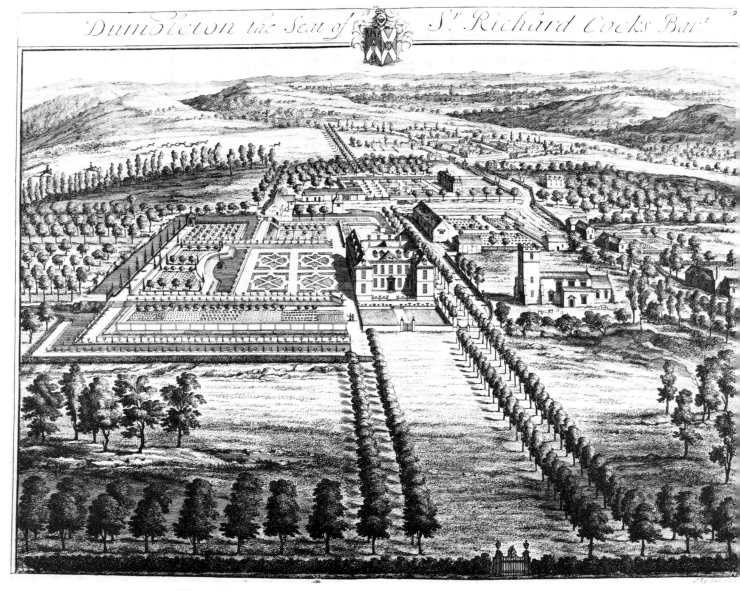

Kip and Knyff's drawing from Britannia Illustrata..., *1707, of Dumbleton, Gloucestershire. The avenues are clearly an addition to an enclosed garden in the Dutch Style.*
Courtesy The British Library.

accounts survive and we can guess that Dorothy Temple's flower garden contained tulips, crocus, polyanthus, gillyflowers (clove-scented pinks and wallflowers), roses, cornflowers, cyclamen, hollyhocks, jasmine, lavender, pansies, poppies, rosemary and violets. The small plants would be used in the knot gardens and the larger plants would be placed against the walls and hedges.

There were no forest trees inside the garden at Moor Park, but the tree-lined avenues outside the garden are very significant. They project outwards into the countryside and thus signpost the future development of English garden design. A careful examination of the avenues in Kip and Knyff's *Britannia Illustrata*[23] reveals that the practice of attaching avenues to enclosed gardens became common in England. Very few of their drawings show a systematic pattern of avenues radiating from a central point. Most are formed by newly planted lines of trees which meet the walls of the enclosed gardens at right angles. The bird's-eye

Westbury Court, Gloucestershire, c.1902. The garden, which is being restored, is the best example in England of a Dutch canal garden.

viewpoint adopted by Kip and Knyff makes these avenues look more radial than they would appear on a plan. Non-radial avenues of this type are shown on the drawing of Dumbleton, Gloucestershire, and were added to Ham House after the plan of the enclosed garden was drawn in 1671 (p.60).

The best surviving examples of the Dutch Style are the canal garden at Westbury Court, which is being restored and, at Levens Hall, the topiary garden (p.57) and the 'informal avenue' which reaches out into the landscape on undulating ground. Since Levens Hall was designed by a Frenchman, Guillaume Beaumont, for a supporter of the Stuart cause, it illustrates the general confusion between French and Dutch influences on English garden design.

CHAPTER III

1714-1810: The Forest, Serpentine
and Irregular Styles

The Forest Style

Royal leadership in the art of garden design began to decline after the accession of George I in 1714. He did not share the Stuart passion for the arts in general or gardens in particular. Artistic leadership passed to the nobles, especially the Whig nobles. This was the beginning of the most creative century in the history of English garden design, and the first of the new styles — the English Forest Style — was characterised by avenues and extensive plantings of forest trees.

The name for the style comes from Stephen Switzer. He was critical of the 'stiff Dutch way' of London and Wise, and wrote a three-volume book on 'the general designing and distributing of country seats into gardens, woods, parks, paddocks, etc., which I therefore call *Forest,* or, in a more easy style Rural Gardening'.[1] Switzer admired the magnificent gardens at Versailles, Marly and Fontainebleau and confessed that ''tis to them I owe a great part of that knowledge I have in the designing part of gardening'.[2] Switzer saw himself as the first English author,

A forest glade at Wrest Park, in Bedfordshire. There was hardly any woodland on site when work started on the garden in 1706. The monument is dedicated to Lancelot Brown who, ironically, was responsible for the destruction of innumerable avenues.

The central avenue at St. Paul's Walden Bury, Hertfordshire.

rather than mere translator, to advocate the French Style. However, he had not visited France and the style which he advocated deserves a separate name. It differs from the French and the Dutch Styles in important respects.

Switzer believed that his style was more economical and more beautiful than the style of London and Wise. He thought more money should be spent on forest planting and that it should be obtained by reducing the size of parterres or by laying them to grass. Since few avenues could be made by cutting through existing woods in England, massive tree planting was essential to create any semblance of the French style. Switzer also believed that money was being wasted on levelling hills and filling dales to comply with a pre-ordained plan. He distrusted paper plans because they often led to the felling of a noble oak 'to humour the regular and delusive schemes of some paper engineer', and he disliked costly garden walls which so often obstructed views of 'the expansive volumes of nature herself'.[3] These comments, from the 1742 edition of *Ichnographia Rustica,* provide an excellent illustration of the way in which the swing from rationalism to empiricism was affecting the art of garden design.

Switzer emerges from his writings as a charming man who may well have played a crucial role in the evolution of English garden design. It is sad that no gardens which he designed are known to be in existence. There are, however, a number of gardens which were made between 1700 and 1750 and illustrate the principles of the Forest Style. The best examples are Bramham Park (1700-31), Cirencester Park (1715-40), St. Paul's Walden Bury (1720-5), and Wrest Park (1706-40). They are quiet rural retreats with extensive woodlands, radiating avenues looking towards distant views and small or non-existent parterres.

The quietness and relative economy of these estates

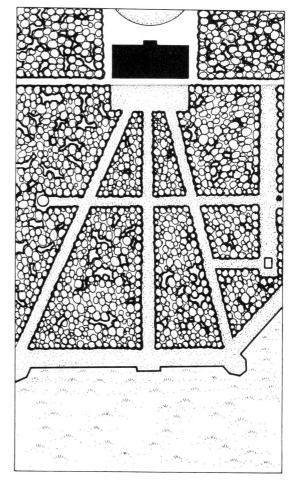

The Forest Style: a simple parterre and avenues running through newly-planted woodland.

indicate another fundamental difference between the French and the Forest Styles: their use. To Louis XIV, Versailles was a symbol of his sun-like magnificence. Power radiated outwards into France from Versailles like the great avenues, and extended to the furthest corners of France. All Louis' subjects were drawn into the orbit of his power and crowds milled through the grounds at Versailles. On festival days there were masques, garden parties and firework displays.

English estates which were laid out in the Forest Style, like Alan Bathurst's park at Cirencester, served a very different purpose. They were intended not for the grandeur of court life but for a Horatian idyll of rural retirement. Switzer described Bathurst as 'the best of Masters, and best of friends', adding that 'the retirement You are pleased to make into your fields and gardens, are evident demonstrations how greatly You prefer solitude before the noise and hurry of public life'.[4] It is not known whether Switzer advised on the design of Cirencester Park but it is perhaps the best surviving example of the Forest Style. Pope was a close friend of Bathurst and had enjoyed a rural life style during his early days in Windsor Forest. He expressed the classical ideal lyrically in his *Ode on Solitude* of 1717:

> Happy the man whose wish and care
> A few paternal acres bound,
> Content to breathe his native air,
> In his own ground.
> Whose herds with milk, whose fields with bread,
> Whose flocks supply him with attire,
> Whose trees in summer yield him shade,
> In winter fire.
> Blest, who can unconcern'dly find
> Hours, days, and years slide soft away,
> In health of body, peace of mind,
> Quiet by day,
> Sound sleep by night; study and ease,

The radiating avenues at Cirencester Park, Gloucestershire. This was a major forestry enterprise and survives as one of the best examples of the English Forest Style.

St. Paul's Walden Bury, Hertfordshire, 1720-5, and Bramham Park,
West Yorkshire, 1700-31, are two of
the finest examples of the Forest Style
in garden design, embracing as they do
the early eighteenth century ideal of
'rural retirement'.

Both the ride at Bramham Park,
right — which centres on the Four
Faces Urn (p. 211) and was intended,
as in modern forestry practice, to give
access for new planting, and the
central avenue at St. Paul's Walden
Bury, above, look towards distant
views.

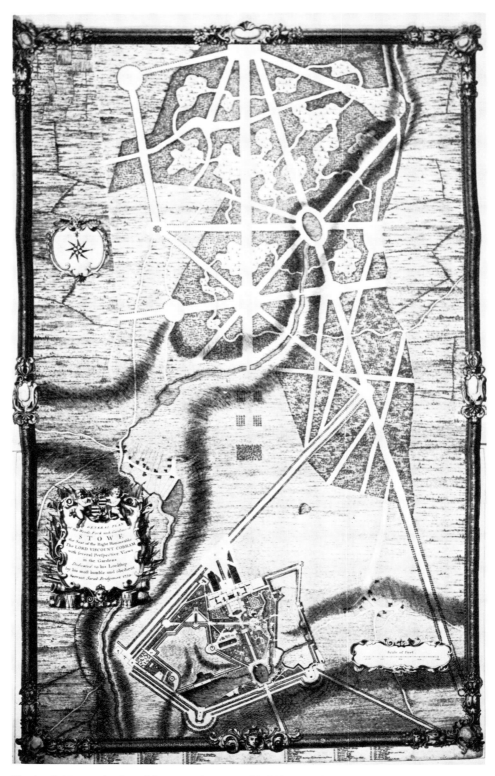

Charles Bridgeman's plan of Stowe, as it appeared in Views of Stowe, *1739, published by Sarah Bridgeman. The area by the house, in the lower part of the plan, contains 'Dutch' canals and parterres, while the upper part derives from the Forest Style.*

Together mixt; sweet recreation;
And Innocence, which most does please
With meditation.

Thus let me live, unseen, unknown,
Thus unlamented let me die,
Steal from the world, and not a stone
Tell where I lie.[5]

This is not at all the life which Louis wished to live at Versailles, nor indeed the life which Charles II wished to live at his London palace gardens.

Bathurst's park at Cirencester was formed almost entirely by new planting. The avenues which radiate from his house were planned according to aesthetic criteria but their function, like modern forestry roads, was to give access to the new plantings. Pope asked 'who plants like Bathurst?' and invested £4,000 at four per cent in his friend's forestry venture.[6] Pope's own garden at Twickenham (p.25) was small by comparison with Cirencester Park, but may be considered an example of the Forest Style. It has avenues and grass but no topiary or parterres. The probability is that Pope was influenced either by Switzer's book or by advice from Switzer's fellow apprentice, Charles Bridgeman.

Bridgeman was a friend of Pope. He shared Switzer's liking for extensive prospects and his willingness to respond to the genius of the place. It is for these reasons that Willis describes Bridgeman as a pioneer in the change 'from the geometric layouts of the early 1700s to the freer designs of Capability Brown'.[7]

Bridgeman's most important project was Stowe. A plan of the park, published by his wife in 1739, the year after his death, shows some features of the Dutch Style, but there is also a network of newly planted avenues which are linked together by a series of bastions. The bastions were characteristic of both

A bastion at Bramham Park, West Yorkshire. Bastions at the edge of the forest, and giving views over farmland, were a characteristic feature of the Forest Style.

Some of the finest eighteenth century gardens were made at a mid-point in the swing from geometry to irregularity. The water garden at Studley Royal, North Yorkshire, has an asymmetrical pattern and is set in a valley which winds round the hill to Fountains Abbey. Courtesy Michael Lancaster.

Characteristic features of the Forest Style were long avenues and bastions. Both allowed for extensive prospects to open country. Left, the long avenue at Castle Howard, North Yorkshire and, above, forest-style bastions at Levens Hall, Cumbria.

William Kent's rill at Rousham, Oxfordshire is a most delightful example of a stylised serpentine curve.
                                                                    Courtesy Marian Thompson.

The grotto at Claremont, Surrey.

Bridgeman and Switzer. They commanded wide views of the surrounding countryside and formed part of the ha-ha (sunk fence) which protected the garden from sheep and cattle. Forest-style bastions can be found at Bramham Park and Levens Hall, and there are examples of long avenues at Castle Howard and Studley Royal.

Bridgeman's and Switzer's desire to open up views was certainly a move towards more natural estate layout. But taste moved quickly. Some of their clients, and all their clients' descendants, were unable to see what was natural about their designs. At Stowe, and elsewhere, all was swept away to make room for later and freer garden designs. There is a parallel with Pope's poetry. It was regarded as 'natural' during his lifetime but came to be described as 'artificial' by Wordsworth and the romantic critics. The poems survive but Pope's garden, like Bridgeman's and Switzer's work, has almost vanished.

The Serpentine Style

The adjective 'serpentine' is used here to describe that famous style which will be forever associated with the names of William Kent and Lancelot 'Capability' Brown. It is also known as the landscape style, the natural style and the English style, but these names will not be used for the reasons explained at the end of Chapter I. Serpentine is not a perfect description either, but it does have the merit of identifying at least one highly characteristic feature of the style: its use of serpentine lines.

The Graeco-Roman theatre at Claremont. Both this and the preceding photograph illustrate the early eighteenth century ideal of recreating the landscape of antiquity, though the theatre was not intended to stage grim or bloody tragedy.

The roots of the new style reach back into the origins of English empiricism, but its first flowering did not come until after Addison's clear formulation of the landscape ideal in 1712 (p.30). The style became a high fashion during the eighteenth century and occurred in three distinct forms, each of which emphasised an aspect of the landscape ideal. The 'Augustan' or 'poetic' phase, which lasted until about 1750, was a serious attempt to recreate the landscape of antiquity both visually and allegorically. It was followed by the 'Brownian' or 'abstract' phase after 1750, in which the imitation of nature's serpentine lines became the ruling passion. Allegory and symbolism were forgotten. The third variety of the Serpentine Style, known as the *ferme ornée,* is the most elusive. It was a theoretically absorbing attempt to make ideal farms in which one could enjoy the blessings of rural retirement in England, as Horace had done in the Sabine Hills. It spanned the eighteenth century, but, since the farms were made by their owners, few plans or other records survive. All three variants will be examined in greater detail later in the chapter.

The steps by which the Serpentine Style arose out of the Forest Style constitute a fascinating episode in the history of taste. It has occupied the attention of many historians and is best chronicled by Christopher Hussey in *English Gardens and Landscapes 1700-1750.* One of the most celebrated steps in the progression was the retention of Wray Wood and Henderskelf Lane at Castle Howard. Hussey

The flowing line was 'Capability' Brown's hallmark and at Stowe, Buckinghamshire, the Grecian Vale is beautifully composed. Brown probably worked with Kent on the design, but it is executed with more feeling for the abstract composition of landform and woods than most of Kent's work.
Courtesy Michael Lancaster.

Kent's garden designs looked back to ancient times, and were replete with statuary, temples and grottoes. At Chiswick House, London, the verdant exedra contains Roman statues, said to have come from Hadrian's villa.

Brown's embankment at Alnwick Castle, Northumberland, has created a romantic park outside the castle walls. It is surprising how much of his design work survives in parks all over England.

Kent's exedra at Stowe, Buckinghamshire, has niches for 'British Worthies' who forever look upwards to the Temple of Ancient Virtue across the Elysian Fields.

85

The low hill on which Wray (or Ray) Wood stands is described by Hussey as 'historic ground, since it became the turning point of garden design not only at Castle Howard but in England'. The old beech wood was felled during the war but the area has been replanted.

comments that the low hill on which they lie is 'historic ground, since it became the turning point of garden design not only at Castle Howard but in England'.[8] He might have added 'and the world'.

The low hill was occupied by an extremely fine stand of mature beech trees. It lies immediately to the east of the new house which Vanbrugh and Hawksmoor designed between 1699 and 1712. George London advised on the layout of the grounds until his death in 1714 and his apprentice, Stephen Switzer, is assumed to have advised Lord Carlisle after London's death. London wished to drive an avenue from the north front of the house up the hill and into Wray Wood. He planned to carve out a network of intersecting avenues inside the beech wood. Switzer wrote in 1718 that London's proposal 'would have spoil'd the Wood, but that his Lordship's superlative genius prevented it'.[9] Wray Wood was retained and furnished with waterworks and labyrinthine paths to make what Switzer judged an 'incomparable Wood the highest pitch that Natural and Polite Gardening can possibly ever arrive to'.[10] Hussey suggests that, since Switzer was both a modest man and an expert in waterworks, it may in fact have been he, rather than Lord Carlisle, who had the idea of conserving Wray Wood. Today the waterworks have gone and the beech wood is recovering after being clear-felled in 1940.

Henderskelf Lane survives intact as the path which skirts the southern flank of Wray Wood and joins Castle Howard to the Temple of Four Winds (p.28). The lane was an ancient track which, according to the logic of George London's layout, should have been eliminated or straightened. In fact, it was retained and made into a broad meandering grassy walk which commands a heroic prospect of the landscape. It resembles the grass terrace at nearby Duncombe, but it is not known which of the two terraces was the first to be made. A visual comparison of the two terraces leads one to think that Henderskelf is the prototype and Duncombe the second version. Thomas Duncombe married a Howard and planned to extend the serpentine walk for three miles along the hillside to Rievaulx in the 1740s. Had the project been implemented it would surely have become the most splendid serpentine promenade in the land.

Henderskelf Lane, according to the logic of London's design, should have been straightened, but the curves were retained, making it one of the first serpentine paths in England.

The grass serpentine terrace at Duncombe, North Yorkshire — another early serpentine walk, possibly inspired by Henderskelf Lane. The terrace wraps round the hillside and commands a fine prospect.

Two examples of the wild, irregular style admired by Sir Uvedale Price at Downton, Shropshire, the estate of his friend Richard Payne Knight. In 1806 Repton described the rough lane opposite as: 'A narrow, wild, and natural path, [which] sometimes ascends to an awful precipice, from when the foaming waters are heard roaring in the dark abyss below, or seen wildly dashing against its opposite banks...' He wrote that 'the path, in various places, crosses the water by bridges of the most romantic and contrasted forms; and...is occasionally varied and enriched by caves and cells, hovels, and covered seats, or other buildings, in perfect harmony with the wild but pleasing horrors of the scene'.

The Serpentine, Hyde Park, London. Bridgeman's design for the single large lake, formed by joining up several smaller areas of water, was one of the important landmarks in the evolution of the Serpentine Style.

Some of the other well-known steps in the evolution of the Serpentine Style include: Vanbrugh's suggestion that £1,000 could be saved by keeping Old Woodstock Manor in Blenheim Park as a picturesque feature in the view; the acceptance of site irregularities at Bramham Park so that the garden has an axis of its own and is not dependent on the axis of the house; the formation of the irregular grove at Melbourne, which Hussey describes as 'the classic example in England of the first movement away from an entirely regular conception of garden design which eventually led to landscape'[11] (as at Bramham the axis of the garden was not related to the axis of the house); the use of the accidental diagonal provided by an old lane at Stowe to form the Great Cross Lime Walk (it crosses at 70° instead of the usual 90°); the extensive use of a ha-ha at Stowe to bring the view of the countryside into the garden; and Charles Bridgeman's design for joining up a series of small ponds in Hyde Park to form the large lake which is now known, appropriately, as The Serpentine.

Each of these evolutionary steps, all of which were taken between 1709 and 1748, marks a slight swing of the pendulum from rationalism to empiricism, from geometrical symmetry and regularity to asymmetry and the use of serpentine curves. Some of the finest eighteenth century gardens were made when the pendulum reached a mid-point between the two poles. Duncombe (1713-50), Studley Royal (1715-30) (p.80), Rousham (1726-39) (p.81) and Stourhead (1726-39) are brilliant examples of the way in which a disciplined and imaginative design concept can be developed from an intuitive response to a sense of place. But it is

Stourhead is the finest example of an ideal landscape in England.

not sufficient to analyse the first phase of the Serpentine Style in geometrical terms alone: it was rich in symbolism, allusion and allegory.

The reason for describing the first phase of the Serpentine Style as the 'Augustan' or 'poetic' phase is that it was closely connected with the English Augustans and their poetry. As Horace and Virgil had celebrated the first Augustan age of peace and security after a period of civil war, so the English Augustans welcomed a second golden age after the troubles of the seventeenth century. Writers, artists, architects, gardeners and a host of others sought to relive and recreate the glories of Rome in the time of its first emperor Augustus, who 'found the city built of brick, and left it built of marble'.[12] Augustus' reign, from 27 B.C. to 14 A.D., saw a great flowering of the arts. In eighteenth century England, Palladian architecture, heroic couplets and the Augustan garden all expressed the desire to look back to a golden age. Alexander Pope was the greatest of the new Augustan poets and had a decisive effect on garden design. He wrote in 1713 that 'the taste of the ancients in their gardens' was for 'the amiable simplicity of unadorned nature, that spreads over the mind a more noble sort of tranquility'.[13] Eighteen years later he devoted an epistle, versified in heroic couplets, to the man who had become the foremost English patron of

The Palladian bridge at Stowe. Eighteenth century England, like sixteenth century Italy, sought to recreate the glory of the ancient world.
Courtesy Frances Bell Macdonald.

Studley Royal, North Yorkshire, 1715-30, marks the mid-point between rationalism (geometrical symmetry) and empiricism (asymmetry). (See also p.80.)

91

Loudon proposed the Irregular Style for Harewood House, West Yorkshire (p.105). His scheme was not implemented, but in 1962 a storm destroyed much of the lakeside planting, part of which is now regenerating in the Irregular Style and thus creating something of the effect which Loudon strove to attain.

The Venus Vale at Rousham, Oxfordshire, designed by Kent. Courtesy Frances Bell Macdonald.

Palladianism, Lord Burlington:

> In you, my Lord, Taste sanctifies Expense,
> For Splendour borrows all her Rays from Sense,
> You show us, Rome was glorious, not profuse,
> And pompous buildings once were things of use.[14]

Burlington's friend and protégé, William Kent, became the foremost Augustan garden designer. It would be folly to attempt a better account of his achievement than Horace Walpole's:

> At that moment appeared Kent, painter enough to taste the charms of landscape, bold and opinionative enough to dare and to dictate, and born with a genius to strike out a great system from the twilight of imperfect essays. He leaped the fence, and saw that all nature was a garden. He felt the delicious contrast of hill and valley changing imperceptibly into each other, tasted the beauty of the gentle swell, or concave scoop, and remarked how loose groves crowned an easy eminence with happy ornament, and while they called in the distant view between their graceful stems, removed and extended the perspective by delusive comparison.[15]

The Arcade, or Praeneste, also at Rousham. As with the Venus Vale, Kent was referring back to antiquity — the Praeneste being named after the place where a Roman oracle resided.
Courtesy Frances Bell Macdonald.

Castle Howard, North Yorkshire. 'The masterpiece of... the Heroic Age of English landscape architecture'.

Kent worked with Bridgeman on some estates, and in succession to Bridgeman on others. The historical records are incomplete, but it is likely that, when they worked together, Kent provided the ideas and Bridgeman the technical expertise. The best surviving examples of their work are at Claremont, Chiswick, Rousham and Stowe. The avenues in these gardens remind us of the Forest Style, and the delightful lakes and glades are amongst the earliest examples of the Serpentine Style. Kent loved to give canals, basins and water bodies a 'natural' shape. In Walpole's words again: 'The gentle stream was taught to serpentise seemingly at its pleasure'.[16] However, Kent's interest was more in seeing landscape as pictures than as plans. 'The great principles on which he worked were perspective, and light and shade',[17] but, as with the landscape painters of his time, the landscape which really interested him was the landscape of antiquity. The gardens designed by Kent and Bridgeman were redolent of ancient times, replete with statuary, temples, grottoes and hermits' caves.

At Chiswick House the statues in the exedra are said to have come from Hadrian's villa and to represent Caesar, Pompey and Cicero (p.84). Another of Kent's exedra, at Stowe, has niches for eight 'British Worthies'. Their derivative genius is shown allegorically by making them look upwards to the Temple of Ancient Virtue set in the Elysian Fields (p.85). The design of the Temple was itself derived from the Temple of Vesta which overlooks the Tivoli gorge outside Rome. At Rousham, Kent designed the Venus Vale and an arcade which was named the Praeneste after the Roman resort where an oracle resided (p.93). At Claremont, Bridgeman designed a Graeco-Roman amphitheatre made out of grass instead of stone — it was not intended as a stage for bloody spectacles (p.83). He placed a circular pond in front of the amphitheatre which Kent changed into the natural lake that occupies the centre of the valley today.

This was the age when garden design was a 'nobleman's recreation', and when many noblemen had a love of antiquity and landscape painting which excelled that of the professional designer. Lord Carlisle was the leading figure in the creation of the park at Castle Howard, which Hussey calls 'the masterpiece of...the Heroic Age of English landscape architecture'.[18] In 1733 the anonymous poet who wrote that '*Carlisle's genius*...form'd this great design' compared Wray Wood to an Italian scene:

> This Wood with Justice *Belvidere* we name.
> Statues at proper Views enrich the Scene,
> Here chaste *Diana* and the *Paphian* Queen,
> Tho' Opposites in Fame, tho' Rivals made
> Contented stand under one common Shade.[19]

The Temple of Four Winds at Castle Howard was inspired by Palladio's Villa Capra which Colen Campbell adapted at Mereworth and Lord Burlington at Chiswick.

Charles Hamilton and Henry Hoare were lesser noblemen who had been on the Grand Tour and acquired a passion for the landscape of antiquity. At Painshill Hamilton installed a Grecian statue of Bacchus in a temple, built a Roman bath house, and assembled a complete set of busts of the Roman emperors.

Henry Hoare II, known in the family as 'the Magnificent', returned from Italy in 1741 to take possession of the Stourhead estate. He made the lake in 1744 and surrounded it with a walk which was conceived as an allegory of Aeneas' voyage after the fall of Troy. The grotto marks a stage of his journey, and the Temple of Flora is inscribed with the caution uttered by the Cumaean Sybil, in Virgil's *Aeneid,* before she led Aeneas into the underworld to hear the prophecy of Rome's founding: 'Begone! you who are uninitiated, begone!'[20] Hoare also based his design for the bridge on Palladio's five-arched bridge at Vicenza and expressed the hope that the whole composition would resemble a painting by Gaspar Poussin.

The second phase of the Serpentine Style was heralded by the start of Lancelot Brown's career as a freelance designer. By 1751 he had been head gardener at Stowe for ten years and had seen great works done there under the overall direction of William Kent. They probably worked together on the design of the Grecian Vale, which had classical overtones but was executed with more feeling for the abstract composition of landform and woods than most of Kent's work (p.84). The serpentine shapes became Brown's hallmark. He was not averse to including the occasional temple when it improved the composition, but there is no

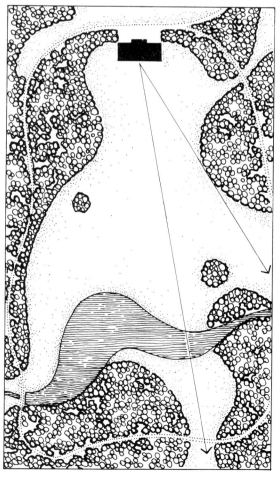

The Serpentine Style: the shapes of the ground, the flooded river valley and perimeter tree belt are based on serpentine curves.

In the Analysis of Beauty, *1753, Hogarth argues that Figure 49, no. 4, shows the 'line of beauty' and that Figure 50, no. 4, shows it 'applied' to the leg of a chair. Figure 53, no. 4 shows it applied to a stay for 'a well formed woman', and Figure 26 shows 'a perfect, precise, serpentine line'. The appreciation of serpentine curves had a profound influence on the design of English gardens.*
Courtesy The British Library.

Brown's Arcadian glade at Prior Park, near Bath, is one of his finest compositions.

reason to think he had any taste for allegory, symbolism or the landscape of ancient Greece and Rome.

During the thirty-two years of his career as an independent designer Brown's style hardly changed and is easily represented by a simple diagram (p.95). It should be thought of as an estate of perhaps one thousand hectares. The most characteristic features of his style are the circular clumps of trees, the grassy meadow in front of the mansion house, the serpentine lake, the enclosing tree belt and the encircling carriage drive. Hussey remarked that Brown was a practical man in the grip of a theory. The diagram shows the theory.

The World, with its finger on the pulse of the nation's taste, was quick to recognise Brown's interest in serpentine shapes and drew a comparison between Hogarth's line of beauty, the profile of a woman's body and a Brownian park. In 1753 the editor wrote that 'a young lady of the most graceful figure I ever beheld' had come to London:

> 'To have her shape altered to the modern fashion'. That is to say, to have her breasts compressed by a flat straight line. I protest, when I saw the beautiful figure that was to be so deformed by the stay maker. I was as much shocked, as if I had been told that she was come to deliver up those animated knolls of beauty to the surgeon — I borrow my terms from gardening, which now indeed furnishes the most pregnant and exalted expressions of any science in being. And this brings to mind the only instance that can give an adequate idea of my concern. Let us suppose that Mr. Brown should, in any one of the many Elysiums he has made, see the old terraces rise again and mask his undulating knolls, or straight rows of trees obscure his noblest configurations of scenery.[21]

The comparison between serpentine lines and women's stays comes from Hogarth's *Analysis of Beauty,* first published in 1753. Hogarth commented that

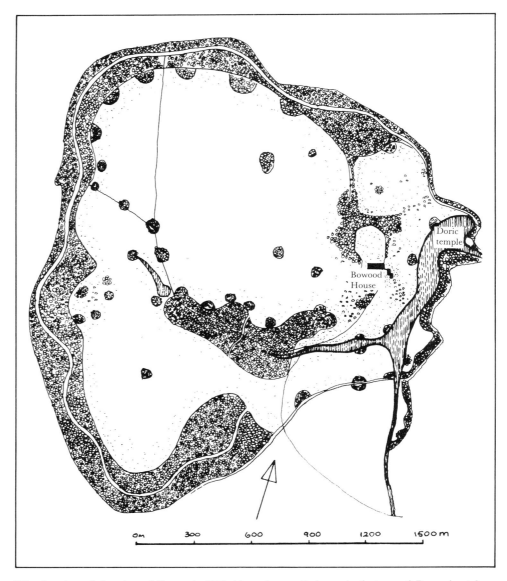

Labels within image: Doric temple, Bowood House, 0m 300 600 900 1200 1500m

The drawing of the plan of Bowood, Wiltshire, shows all the main features of Brown's style.

'there is an elegant degree of plumpness to the skin of the softer sex', and drew diagrams to show how the ideal stay resembled the line of beauty.[22] The beautiful Lady Luxborough borrowed William Shenstone's copy of the book and envied the shape of the letter with which his name began. She wrote in 1754 that she was 'sorry I have not now an S in my name to claim any share in it'.[23] Shenstone's own park at The Leasowes attracted many famous visitors and prevented him from visiting Lady Luxborough as often as she would have liked.

Dorothy Stroud lists 211 designs for English parks which are known to be by, or attributed to, Capability Brown,[24] and a surprising number remain in good condition, often because they have adapted well to modern use as public parks, farms, golf courses and schools. The best of them are magnificent, probably more so today than when seen by Brown's critics in the 1790s. The author's favourites are the Arcadian glade at Prior Park (p.97), the Grecian Vale at Stowe (p.84), the lakes at Luton Hoo and Blenheim, the embankment outside Alnwick Castle

Bowood survives as one of the most complete Brownian parks. The Doric temple is on the north east shore of the lake, as indicated on the plan opposite.

(p.85), the riverside scenery at Chatsworth and the grand views at Petworth and Harewood which J.M.W. Turner painted.

Some of Brown's other designs are so 'natural' and 'English' that it is difficult to appreciate them without a survey of the site as it was and a plan of the work executed. Brown's lakes lie in comfortable depressions, his woods clothe hills which would resist the plough, and his green pastures roll to the rhythm of the English countryside. A large collection of Brown's professional papers, which might have provided more information on what he actually did, was given to Repton by Brown's son but unfortunately it has since disappeared. This paucity of documentation on so many sites makes Bowood a park of special interest. Here the plan and the estate survive in good condition. There is a small Doric temple which has been attributed to Brown[25] on the edge of the lake.

The third variant of the Serpentine Style, known as the *ferme ornée,* is of particular interest to historians of the rural retirement theme. Maren-Sofie Røstvig comments that 'Instead of penning yet another version of Horace's second epode, Southcote translated the literary ideal into a living reality'[26] at Woburn Farm near Chertsey (c.1735). It was a working farm ornamented with trees, shrubs and temples, and is usually described as a *ferme ornée,* despite the fact that Switzer did not introduce the term until 1742. *Ornée* does not convey adequately the fact that these farms were intended to satisfy the widest possible range of human needs and aspirations. An 'ideal farm' would be a better description. The term *ferme ornée* was first applied to The Leasowes in 1746, but it is significant that Shenstone did not include it in the threefold classification of types of gardening which he made in 1764 (kitchen gardening, parterre gardening,

Ideal Skeleton of the Surface of Tew Lodge Farm, made in order to shew the direction of the Roads

Fig 4

Summer or Empty Cart Road

Winter or Loaded Cart Road

Level Road

Fig 5

Hill Side Road

Loudon's design for a ferme ornée *at Great Tew, Oxfordshire. The designer believed that 'time alone is requisite to render Tew Lodge the most magnificent* ferme ornée *in England'. In recent times it has been neglected.*
Courtesy The British Library.

and landskip gardening[27]). He refers to Burke in the following paragraph and it may be that Burke's empiricist aesthetics discouraged Shenstone from using the term. Burke believed there was no connection between use and beauty, and pointed out that the wedge-like snout of a pig and the bared teeth of a wolf are useful but not beautiful.[28] Shenstone may have thought the utility of his farm would be judged a detraction from its beauty.

In practice use *was* combined with beauty on many estates laid out in the Serpentine Style. They were run as ideal farms, whatever the aesthetic beliefs of their owners and designers. This fact was apparent to the French observer R.-L. Girardin whose *Essay on Landscape . . . ,1783*, became popular in England. He greatly admired The Leasowes and wrote:

> This change of things then, from a forced arrangement to one that is easy and natural will bring us back to a true taste for beautiful nature, tend to the increase of agriculture, the propagation of cattle, and, above all, to more humane and salutary regulations of the country, by providing for the subsistence of those whose labour supports the men of more thinking employments who are to instruct or defend society.[29]

J.C. Loudon took these remarks to heart and, at the beginning of the nineteenth century, he redesigned a farm at Great Tew in Oxfordshire. On completing the project he believed that 'time alone is requisite to render Tew Lodge the most magnificent *ferme ornée* in England'.[30] He must have thought his belief well justified when he sold the lease, after four years' work, and made the magnificent profit of £15,000. Like The Leasowes, the farm survives and deserves to be fully restored as a monument to the fact that farmers need not sacrifice beauty to profit. Loudon drained the land, improved the shapes of the fields, made new roads, planted new hedgerows, and strengthened the old tree belt on the skyline to create a delightfully secluded valley.

Flowering plants were an important component of the *ferme ornée* and, as John Harris has pointed out,[31] they were not excluded from the Serpentine Style to the

Weſtwick *in Norfolk, the* Seat *of* John Berney Petre *Eſqr.*

Engraving from Watt's Seats of the Nobility and Gentry, *1782. Like all Watts' illustrations it shows a house surrounded by grass and trees with no sign of any terraces, avenues or parterres.* Courtesy The British Library.

degree which has been supposed. A main feature of Woburn Farm, Surrey, was a walk planted with broom, roses, lilac, columbine, paeonies and sweet william, which wound its way through the fields.[32] Similarly, Shenstone wrote to Lady Luxborough that he had a copy of Philip Miller's *Gardener's Dictionary* and that 'if there arrive a flowering shrub; it is a day of rejoicing with me'.[33] Loudon had an enormous collection of flowering plants at Tew Lodge, and there is a superficial resemblance between his drawings of the garden and the paintings by Thomas Robbins which Harris has used so effectively to establish the presence of flower gardens in eighteenth century estates.

The astonishing degree to which the Serpentine Style was adopted between 1740 and 1780 can be seen by comparing the engravings in Kip and Knyff's *Britannia Illustrata* with those in Watts' *Seats of the Nobility and Gentry.* Kip and Knyff show every house surrounded by walled gardens with no forest trees in the enclosures. Watts shows every house in a grazed field with forest trees approaching the house and framing the view.

The popularity of the Serpentine Style reached fever pitch in the 1780s. Its creators believed their style to be completely natural, but the next generation disagreed. A further move to empiricism brought thoughts of a new style.

The Irregular Style

Travellers were frightened by wild scenery at the beginning of the eighteenth century. When passing through the Alps they would shut their eyes or pull down the blinds in their coaches to hide the jagged cliffs, the torrents, and the imminent prospect of being catapulted over a precipice. By the century's end this fear had so far diminished that a positive liking for 'Salvator Rosa and Sublimity'[34] had taken its place. Travellers sought for ever-wilder places, and garden designers

A 'terrifying' alpine scene: the Devil's Bridge on the old St. Gotthard Pass. As the eighteenth century progressed, the emotions aroused by the passage of the Alps changed from fear to excitement.
Courtesy Swiss National Tourist Office.

A scene, below left, from Salvator Rosa as illustrated in The English Landscape Garden. Frank Clark wrote that 'scandalous legends of lawlessness' became encrusted around the artist who was 'the outlaw and friend' of the banditti who threatened the safety of travellers.   Courtesy Marjorie Clark.

A photograph, below, of the Bernese Alps which shows the scenic splendour which eighteenth century tourists came to appreciate.
Courtesy Swiss National Tourist Office.

A 'sublime' scene in North Wales. The appreciation of wild scenery in Britain developed after the appreciation of alpine scenery.

responded to their new visual taste. In the 1790s they invented the Irregular Style, and in the century which followed they made 'wild', 'rock', and 'woodland' gardens to accommodate plants from far-flung lands and 'the eaves of the world'.[35]

The taste for wild scenery was partly a result of the Grand Tour through Northern Europe to Italy. As the eighteenth century progressed the passage of the Alps gradually changed from a genuinely terrifying experience to one which induced awe and fear at the time, but which could be recalled at home with excitement and youthful pride at dangers overcome. The effects of alpine scenery on the traveller and on garden design were of special interest to Frank Clark:

> For what in fact the gardeners were trying to do...was to recapture the emotions experienced during the Grand Tour when, after leaving the sunny plains of France and Italy, they had ascended the Alps to the very roof of Europe. Suspended between earth and sky they had seen with fearful fascination the complex pattern of the earth at their feet. Mountains, roaring cascades, the evidences of the convulsive forces of nature in these vast ranges, filled them with sensations of awe which they never afterwards forgot. The painter who had best been able to translate this experience into the idiom of paint was Salvator Rosa. Rosa, or Savage Rosa, as he was called... became the romantic hero, the pre-Byronic hero, of the age. His canvases, peopled with hermits and banditti and filled with twisted trees, tumbled rocks, cliffs, ruins and racing skies, enabled the traveller to re-experience the delightful horror of such scenery and to appreciate its significance when met with in poetry, the paintings of other artists and in landscape. The correct link was made by Walpole in a letter during his tour with Gray in 1739: 'Precipices, mountains, torrents, wolves, rumblings, Salvator Rosa!'[36]

The taste for wild scenery at home developed later. It was fostered by William Gilpin (1724-1804), the 'Master of the Picturesque and Vicar of Boldre'.[37] Gilpin's great series of *Picturesque Tours,* published between 1782 and 1809, awakened English tourists to the rugged delights of the River Wye, North Wales and 'the Mountains and Lakes of Cumberland and Westmorland'.[38] His descriptions of picturesque scenery were followed by three essays which reached to the intellectual heart of eighteenth century garden design theory: landscape painting and the appreciation of nature. They were entitled *Three Essays on Picturesque Beauty, on Picturesque Travel and on Sketching Landscape.* Gilpin was critical of smoothness but loved rough scenery — both in the wilds and in gardens:

> But altho the picturesque traveller is seldom disappointed with *pure nature,* however rude, yet we cannot deny, but he is often offended with the productions of art...He is frequently disgusted also, when art aims more at beauty than she ought. How flat, and insipid is often the garden scene, how puerile, and absurd! the banks of the river, how smooth, and parallel! the lawn, and its boundaries, how unlike nature![39]

He also suggested that if a landscape painter wished to paint a garden scene then he would have to:

> Turn the lawn into a piece of broken ground: plant rugged oaks instead of flowering shrubs: break the edges of the walk: give it the rudeness of a road: mark it with wheel tracks; and scatter around a few stones, and brushwood; in a word, instead of making the whole *smooth,* make it *rough;* and you make it also *picturesque.*[40]

Since Claude treated the foregrounds of his paintings in this way, Gilpin took it that the correctness of his taste was established beyond all reasonable doubt.

Sir Uvedale Price was deeply impressed by Gilpin's aesthetic ideas and wished to find a way of applying them to gardens as well as to landscape painting. The title of Price's first book on garden design was *An essay on the Picturesque, as compared with the Sublime and the Beautiful; and, on the use of studying pictures, for the purpose of improving real landscape.* As the title implies, Price believed that the art of laying out real landscape should be based on a study of paintings and natural scenery. He echoed Gilpin's opinion that 'whoever views objects with a painter's eye, looks with indifference, if not disgust, at the clumps, the belts, the made water, and the eternal smoothness and sameness of a finished place'.[41] Price speculated that Lancelot Brown would have thought the 'finest composition of Claude...comparatively rude and imperfect...though he probably might allow...that it had "capabilities" '![42]

Price championed the idea of making wild romantic gardens. He thought it impractical to make them sublime in Burke's sense of 'fitted...to excite the ideas of pain and danger',[43] but entirely feasible to make them picturesque in the sense of rough, varied, and intricate (pp.88 and 89). He hated 'the tameness of the poor pinioned trees of a gentleman's plantation'[44] and artificial lanes with uniform curves. His love was for old country lanes and by-roads in which the ground:

> Is as much varied in form, tint and light and shade as the plants that grow upon it...The winter torrents, in some places wash down the mould from the upper grounds and form projections...with the most luxuriant vegetation; in other parts they tear the banks into deep hollows, discovering the different strata of earth, and the shaggy roots of trees.[45]

Price even thought that 'the tracks of the wheels contribute to the picturesque

Loudon's design for converting the lakeshore at Harewood House from the Serpentine to the Irregular Style. The proposal was not based on an accurate site survey, but Loudon's design intentions are very clear. The plate on p.92 shows the lake in 1984.

effect of the whole'.[46] These were the effects which Price wished to create in gardens. However, he acknowledged that:

> Near the house picturesque beauty must . . . be sacrificed to neatness . . . It is not necessary to model a gravel walk or drive after a sheep track or a cart rut, *though very useful hints may be taken from them both.*[47]

Price's friend and neighbour, Richard Payne Knight, was a less cautious man

J. Loudon, delt.   J. Greig, sculp.

View of Barnbarrow from the East, as it appeared in 1805.

— and extremely rich. At Downton Castle 'large fragments of stone were irregularly thrown amongst briers and weeds, to imitate the foreground of a picture'.[48] According to Repton this was an 'experiment', but J.C. Loudon must have seen it some ten years later and reported that fragments of rock were still 'scattered in front of Downton Castle...quite unconnected with each other'.[49] In his maturity Knight decided that it was more convenient to have a neat terrace in front of his castle. Downton Vale is a very Gilpinesque place and one of the most romantic estates in England. The estate, and Knight's views on terraces, will be further described in the next chapter (p.124).

The young Loudon was an ardent admirer of Price, Knight and total irregularity. He announced to the world in his first book:

> I believe that I am the first who has set out as a landscape gardener, professing to follow Mr. Price's principles. How far I shall succeed in executing my plans, and introducing more of the picturesque into improved places, time alone must determine.[50]

Loudon was the son of a Scots farmer and had not been on a Grand Tour when he arrived in London at the age of twenty. However, he did have memories of the picturesque charm of the Water of Leith in Edinburgh, and of a park outside Edinburgh which had been laid out by a pupil of Lancelot Brown. A tree belt hid the view of Craigmillar Castle and Arthur's Seat, and the brook which ran through the estate had, as Walter Scott later observed, been 'twisted into the links of a string of pork sausages'.[51] Scott, the arch romantic, was also an admirer of Price and Knight. When judged by the principles of Price and Knight, Loudon complained that Brown's style was 'productive of the most tiresome monotony joined to the most disgusting formality'.[52]

Loudon's early work shows his interpretation of Price and Knight's plea for the picturesque. His mentors drew no plans but their admirer was a superb draughtsman. The sketches and plans which he published in *Country Residences* show 'Mr. Brown's style' and 'the modern style' as practised by himself (p.41). It is plain that 'the modern style' is more deserving of the description 'irregular'

View of Barnbarrow from the East, as it will appear when the alterations at present executing have been three years completed.

Above, Loudon's design for converting the Barnbarrow estate to the Irregular Style was to be achieved by making the architecture and planting wild and irregular. Below, Barnbarròch, as it is now known, is even more irregular in its decay than in Loudon's wild design.

than any other style in the history of English garden design. Loudon employed the Irregular Style for a large number of commissions in the first decade of his professional life, and published designs for numerous country residences, including Ditchley Park in Oxfordshire, Harewood House in Yorkshire and Barnbarrow (now Barnbarroch) (pp.106 and 107). Next to nothing survives of his work, but on some estates, including the grounds of Barnbarroch (p.107) and parts of the lakeshore at Harewood (p.92), nature has been allowed to take her course and has created some of the effects which Loudon wished to attain by art.

The Irregular Style had a profound influence on planting design. It offered a theory about the use of foreign plants in English gardens and provided a system of compositional principles which could be used to harmonise exotic and native plants.

Book III of Knight's poem *The Landscape* has a versified discussion of planting design, from which it is clear that Knight was enchanted by the romance of the English landscape:

> O waft me hence to some neglected vale;
> Where, shelter'd, I may court the western gale;
> And, 'midst the gloom which native thickets shed,
> Hide from the noontide beams my aching head!
> For though in British woods no myrtles blow...
> No prowling tiger from the covert springs;
> No scaly serpent, in vast volumes roll'd,
> Darts on the unwary loiterer from his hold.[53]

He liked to see some plants growing in luxuriant good health and with no signs

Oak trees growing in the natural way which Knight admired.

Rhododendrons — 'choice American plants' — at Scotney Castle, Kent. Price was the first author to advocate the use of exotic flowering shrubs outside the confines of the walled garden.

of regret for 'the comforts of a warmer sky'. This led him to prefer 'trees which nature's hand has sown' or which had adapted themselves to the British climate. His favourite trees were the English stalwarts, oak and beech:

> Let then of oak your general masses rise,
> Wher'er the soil its nutriment supplies:
> But if dry chalk and flints, or thirsty sand,
> Compose the substance of your barren land,
> Let the light beech its gay luxuriance shew,
> And o'er the hills its brilliant verdure strew.[54]

Should time or fortune damage an ancient oak then Knight wished to keep its gnarled remains as one would a ruined abbey:

> If years unnumber'd, or the lightning's stroke
> Have bared the summit of the lofty oak
> (Such as, to decorate some savage waste,
> Salvator's flying pencil often traced),
> Entire and sacred let the ruin stand.[55]

Despite his love for native plants, Knight wished to see exotic plants in gardens

The stone for the nineteenth century house at Scotney Castle, Kent, was taken from the garden and the quarry made into an irregular garden planted according to the principles of Sir Uvedale Price.

— providing they were planted near the house or near water and not in the midst of a natural wood:

> The bright acacia, and the vivid plane,
> The rich laburnum with its golden chain;
> And all the variegated flowering race,
> That deck the garden, and the shrubbery grace,
> Should near to buildings, or to water grow,
> Where bright reflections beam with equal glow,
> And blending vivid tints with vivid light,
> The whole in brilliant harmony unite...
> But better are these gaudy scenes display'd
> From the high terrace or rich balustrade;
> 'Midst sculptured founts and vases, that diffuse,
> In shapes fantastic, their concordant hues.[56]

Knight's exposition of the principles for selecting and using plant species was complemented by Price's ideas on how they should be composed to produce a 'brilliant harmony' with 'concordant hues'.

Price was the first author to write openly in favour of using exotic flowering

A rock garden in Birkenhead Park, Cheshire. It is neglected, but not very wild. Paxton designed the park and Edward Kemp became the superintendent.

shrubs outside the narrow confines of the walled garden. He said that if the improver seeks 'an infinite number of pleasing and striking combinations' then he should 'avail himself of some of those beautiful, but less common flowering and climbing plants'.[57] Plantings of furze, wild roses and woodbine might, he suggests, be enlivened with 'Virginia creeper, pericoloca, trailing arbutus' and 'the choice American plants...such as kalmias and rhododendrons'. Although Price was willing to allow flowering plants to be moved from their traditional positions 'in borders or against walls', he insisted that they should be grouped to form painterly compositions. The painters he most admired were Claude, Poussin and Rosa, and he believed that the eye of

A design by Edward Kemp for a quarry garden. The rough stone adds to the ruggedness of the scene.

The Irregular Style: all the lines are broken and irregular in the highest degree.

the landscape painter, with its understanding of nature and the principles of composition, was the best guide to good planting design. This idea assumed great importance during the nineteenth century and resulted in the romantic woodland gardens which now grace so many of England's stately homes. Scotney Castle in Kent is an outstanding example. Christopher Hussey writes that it was planted by his grandfather as a deliberate application of the principles of Sir Uvedale Price.[58]

The Irregular Style is of great interest as an extreme application of the idea that art should imitate nature. As can be seen from the drawing above it made great use of irregular lines and represents the furthest possible remove from geometrical regularity. Had the Irregular Style ever become popular as a plan style, as well as a planting style, it might have shielded Brown from the nineteenth century criticism that he imitated nature too closely and that his plans were too formal.

CHAPTER IV

1794-1870: The Transition, Italian and Mixed Styles

The Transition Style

The Transition Style is arguably the greatest in the history of English garden and landscape design: it combined the best of eighteenth century landscape practice into one magnificent whole. The theory on which the style rests is often described as 'picturesque' because it requires the composition of landscape scenery into a foreground, a middleground and a background. The idea was applied to country estates by making a terrace as a 'beautiful' foreground, and then forming a 'transition' to a 'picturesque' park, and beyond to a 'sublime' background which could be a mountain range, an ocean, a river, a forest or a distant view.

Sir Uvedale Price, 1747-1829.

The Transition Style is also the chief support for the claim that English landscape designers made a unique contribution to western culture during the eighteenth century. Several proponents of the claim were mentioned in the Preface. Nikolaus Pevsner's name can be added to their number. In his 1955 Reith Lectures Pevsner identified an 'English picturesque theory' which 'lies hidden in the writings of the improvers from Pope to Uvedale Price and Payne Knight' as the foundation for an 'English national planning theory'.[1] Pevsner asserted that the theory gave English planners 'something of great value to offer to other nations', and asked whether 'the same can be said of painting, of sculpture, and of architecture proper?'[2] His answer was that Henry Moore and other sculptors had 'given England a position in European sculpture such as she has never before held', but that contemporary painting and architecture were of a lower order of excellence.

A large body of design theory was developed to support the Transition Style, and its influence outside the realm of garden design has been amazing.[3] The first and most obvious application of the theory was to architecture. It provided a rationale for irregular planning to accommodate a building's functional requirements, and for the design of buildings as a pictorial contribution to the scenery. When applied to urban design, the theory led to the picturesque planning of streets to create a sequence of visual experiences, as for example Nash's Regent Street in London. When applied to planning, the theory produced the idea that there should be a grand transition from an urban city centre, through healthy suburbs and a green belt, through a rural landscape which is protected from urban sprawl, and finally to the national parks, undeveloped coasts and other natural places. From the perspective of the 1980s the picturesque theory can be seen as a precursor of the conservation movement: it provided sound reasons for preserving ancient buildings, for conserving natural vegetation and for designing new buildings which fit well into their surroundings.

113

In geometrical terms the Transition Style made use of elements which derive from four earlier styles of English garden design: the foreground terrace came from the Enclosed Style, the taste for extensive prospects from the Forest Style, the middleground park from the Serpentine Style, and the background scenery from the Irregular Style.

The first hint that these ideas could be combined came from William Gilpin. He included the following observation in his *Remarks on Forest Scenery,* 1791:

> As the park is an appendage of the house, it follows that it should participate of its neatness, and elegance. Nature, in all her great walks of landscape, observes this accommodating rule. She seldom passes abruptly from one mode of scenery to another; but generally connects different species of landscape by some third species, which participates of both. A mountainous country rarely sinks immediately into a level one; the swellings and heavings of the earth grow gradually less. Thus, as the house is connected with the country through the medium of the park, the park should partake of the neatness of the one, and of the wildness of the other.[4]

Humphry Repton,
1752-1818

Gilpin's remark was taken up and developed by three great landscape theorists: Sir Uvedale Price, Richard Payne Knight and Humphry Repton. Their writings look back on the literature and practice of the eighteenth century and form the starting point from which all nineteenth century theorists began their consideration of the subject.

Price and Knight were wealthy landowners, old friends and neighbours in Herefordshire and Shropshire. Repton came from Norfolk and met the other two as a result of an invitation to design an estate at Ferney Hall in Herefordshire which belonged to a friend of Knight. The three friends were each preparing to publish books on landscape design in the year 1794.[5] Knight was first off the mark and hurried the others into print. Repton succeeded in getting his book printed in 1794, but did not manage to publish until early in the following year because he required the services of a small army of women and children to colour up his engravings. The measure of agreement between the opinions expressed by the three men was considerable and a modern textbook editor might have persuaded them to put their names to a single treatise. The sparkle of individuality would have been lost, but the three would surely have agreed if they had had any conception of how seriously readers were going to overstate their differences and misunderstand their writings.

Many of the differences between Price, Knight and Repton can, in fact, be removed by distinguishing between the specialised and ordinary meanings of the words 'beautiful', 'sublime' and 'picturesque'. In the remainder of this book the words will be written with a capital letter when they are used in a special eighteenth century sense. Thus Beautiful will refer to smoothness, delicacy and gradual variation, Sublime to the great, terrible and awe-inspiring, and

Picturesque to the intermediate aesthetic category of roughness, wildness and irregularity. When using the words in their modern sense they will be written with the first letter in the lower case. *The Concise Oxford Dictionary* defines beautiful as 'delighting the eye', sublime as 'so distinguished by elevation or size or nobility or grandeur or other impressive quality as to inspire awe or wonder', and picturesque as 'fit to be the subject of a striking picture'. The meaning of sublime has undergone the least change.

In order to bring out the points of agreement between the three men and avoid the anachronism of a modern technical editor, we can consider the advice which they might have given to a mutual friend who had recently inherited a country seat. (Knight and Price occasionally gave advice to their friends but did not make a charge for it. Repton was an impoverished squire who asked a fee for his advice and summarised his opinion in beautiful hand-written volumes illustrated with his own watercolours and bound in red morocco leather. They were known as Red Books.) Let us assume then, that having come into possession of a five hundred hectare estate in 1795, a mutual friend has asked the three literary squires for their opinion on how to improve his estate in the contemporary taste. Their collective advice can be expressed in modern English except for the words Beautiful, Sublime and Picturesque:

Richard Payne Knight, 1750-1824.

> Good morning. We have completed a thorough study of your estate and Mr. Repton has made sketches from numerous points of view in order fully to appraise its present character. The changes which we propose will be designed to fit in with the existing site and to make improvements which will create a landscape which is both useful and beautiful.
>
> It is highly desirable that there should be a smooth transition between your house and the natural landscape. We can best explain this idea by referring to the work of the great landscape painters from whom we have learnt our aesthetics (pp.118 and 119). The foreground of the view from your house should be a terrace garden with a profusion of flowers. It should be Beautiful and well kept for your family's use, with something of the character of a garden scene by Watteau or, if you decide to have a lake, a Claudian seaport. The middleground of the view should be a noble park, laid out with a view to Picturesque effect but available for agricultural use. Claude and Poussin often show how Picturesque scenes can be when they contain sheep and herdsmen. The background of your view should be Sublime and we recommend felling some trees to open up a view of the waterfall and the forest scenery. You have the makings of a Salvator Rosa on the edge of your estate and should most certainly keep the ancient oak and shepherd's cottage which lie at the foot of the hill.
>
> Each of the three grounds in the scene can contain more than one of the aesthetic qualities, but the Beautiful should predominate in the foreground, the Picturesque in the middleground and the Sublime in the background. Nature shows us how to combine the qualities when we see the Beauty of

Repton wrote: 'The aspect of a house requires the first consideration, since no beauty of prospect can compensate for the cold exposure to the north, the glaring blaze of a setting sun, or the frequent boisterous winds and rains from the west and south-west'. He often recommended sites on rising ground, but well below the crest of a hill, as in this proposal for Bayham Abbey, Kent.

a rose set off by the Picturesque setting of its sharp thorns and serrated leaves. We can also learn from nature and from the landscape painters how best to combine unity with variety. New planting will unify the scene, like the light of the setting sun. It will also provide shelter from the strong south westerly winds.

You will require a new mansion and it should be very carefully sited to have a good microclimate and to command fine views. The house should dominate the foreground but should only be an incident in the background which contributes to the scenery. Lancelot Brown was too much interested in the middleground, but he had excellent taste in the selection of sites and in the composition of land and woods to make a middleground for the view. It is very important that a balance should be achieved between the competing demands of prospect and aspect: a good view is pleasant but a good microclimate is essential. A well designed garden will lengthen the summer by catching the winter sun and keeping out cold winds. It should also contain shady groves in which the family can relax on hot afternoons.

The principle of association which has helped us to plan the grounds should also be used to guide the design of your house. It should look like a building which belongs to the age, country and place in which it will be built. The materials should be of a colour and texture which suit the style and the site — preferably a local stone. Since all the rooms and outbuildings should be planned to meet the needs of your family and servants, we think that an irregular floor plan is more convenient than strict symmetry.

The next task is to select an architectural style. We often think that an Italian style is best for a Claudian site, a Grecian style for a Poussinesque site and an English style for a typically English site. It is also important for your house to look its part; it should not resemble a church, a university or a temple. Since your estate is near the Welsh border and your house will be larger than a manor house but smaller than a palace, we think that the English castle style would be a very appropriate choice.

'Let us have a small temple in the park where we can join you... on hot summer days'. At Hatchlands, Surrey, there is a transition from the terrace to the temple. Both were designed in the 1920s — though Repton produced a Red Book for the estate c.1797.

Repton's sketch of Prospect Hill at Longleat where 'parties are permitted to bring their refreshments; which circumstance tends to enliven the scene... and to mark the liberality of its noble proprietor'. Courtesy The British Library.

Three landscape paintings which reflect the Transition Style as propounded by Price, Knight and Repton. Above: 'The foreground should be Beautiful and well kept like a garden scene by Watteau'. Le Bal Champêtre *by Antoine Watteau (1684-1721). Opposite top: 'The middleground should be a Picturesque parkland scene of the type painted by Claude and Poussin. The farm animals will make it more Picturesque'.* Jacob with Laban and his Daughters *by Claude Lorrain (1600-82). Opposite: 'The background should be a Sublime scene of the type painted by Salvator Rosa'.* River Landscape with Apollo and the Sibyl *by Salvator Rosa (1615-73).*

Watteau and Claude reproduced by permission of the Governors of Dulwich Picture Gallery.

Rosa reproduced by permission of the Trustees, The Wallace Collection, London.

119

The Transition Style: the plan moves from a geometrical terrace, through a serpentine middleground to an irregular background.

'The mouldering remnants of obsolete taste and fallen magnificence'. The quote is from Knight, but the drawing of a Picturesque ruin comes from the 1842 edition of Price's Essays. Courtesy The British Library.

John Ruskin's drawing of Abstract Lines (from The Stones of Venice, *Vol. 1, 1851) was used to show that all the most beautiful curves derive from nature. Curve ab comes from the Aiguille de Blaitière; curve h is from a branch, and curves qr are from leaf shapes. In the nineteenth century it was accepted that all the curves which exist in nature can have a place in landscape design (p.37). Ruskin wrote that 'the lines of nature are alike in all her works . . . their universal property being that of ever-varying curvature in the most subtle and subdued transition'.*

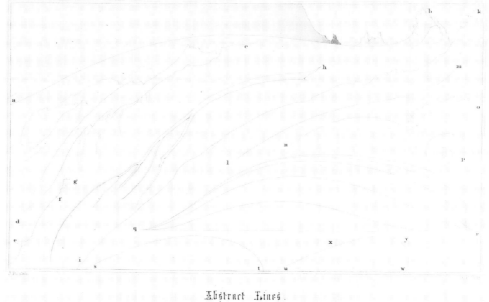

Abstract Lines.

Your estate is large and we have suggested the incorporation of many different sources of pleasure into the layout. It would therefore be delightful to have a circuitous carriage drive. When driving round the estate you and your visitors will be able to experience all the views and qualities which we have aimed to create: congruity, utility, order, symmetry, picturesque effects, intricacy, simplicity, variety, novelty, contrast, continuity, association, appropriation, animation, grandeur and the ever-changing effects of the seasons, the weather and the times of day.

Finally, let us have a small temple in the park where we can join you for an outdoor meal or drink on hot summer days. It should be sited on the brow of the hill which can be seen from your drawing room window, and we suggest that you inscribe it with the famous lines by Alexander Pope which have guided us in the design of your estate:

> To build, to plant, whatever you intend,
> To rear the Column, or the Arch to bend,
> To swell the Terras, or to sink the Grot;
> In all, let *Nature* never be forgot.
> Consult the *Genius* of the *Palace* in all
> That tells the waters or to rise, or fall...
> Joins willing woods, and varies shades from shades,
> Now Breaks, or now directs, th'intending Lines;
> *Paints* as you plant, and as you work, *Designs*.

There are eleven key ideas embodied in the above advice on estate layout: existing character, nature, utility, the transition, landscape painting, planting, unity in variety, the balance of prospect and aspect, appropriation, irregular architecture and the principle of association. If the three squires' views were set out individually and then compared, we would find some cases of complete agreement, some of differing emphasis and some of near disagreement.

They would have been in complete agreement over the importance of existing character, nature, planting, irregular architecture and the combination of unity with variety.

Cases of differing emphasis would be found over prospect and aspect, appropriation, the transition and the principle of association. Repton[6] and Price[7] give the fullest accounts of how to form a transition between the terrace and wild nature. Repton was the first of the three to propose the reintroduction of terraces (p.129) to English gardens,[8] but the demand for a paved area near the house had been growing since the 1750s. In 1771 even the *Encyclopaedia Britannica* had advised that 'regularity is required in that part of a garden which joins the dwelling house',[9] but the paved area was recommended for purely utilitarian reasons. Price and Knight were the first to argue on *visual* grounds that a terrace would be an asset in composing the foreground of the view. Repton originally recommended terraces for utility but came to agree with his friends on this point.

From 1794 onwards each of the three advocated a transition from regularity to wildness. As can be seen in the diagram opposite, the transition runs from a regular terrace beside the house, through a serpentine park to a wild forest or other sublime feature. Repton, as the only professional designer in the trio, has the best advice on how to achieve a balance between a good prospect and a good

Knight persuaded the owner of Powis Castle, Powys, to keep the terraces which step down the hillside. He believed that a terrace created a foreground to a view.

microclimate.[10] He was also, perhaps for the same reason, the only one to recommend the idea of appropriation.[11]

Knight, as the most philosophically able, gives most attention to the principle of association which underlies each author's aesthetic views. Knight believed that our aesthetic judgement of phenomena is governed by our understanding of their associations, history and symbolic significance. For example:

> Ruined buildings, with fragments of sculptured walls and broken columns, the mouldering remnants of obsolete taste and fallen magnificence, afford pleasure to every learned beholder, imperceptible to the ignorant, and wholly independent of their real beauty.[12].

The cases of near disagreement between Repton, Price and Knight would have arisen over their interpretation of utility and landscape painting. These disagreements have received considerable attention from commentators but are of much more philosophical than practical consequence. They turn on the precise meaning and significance given to the words 'picturesque' and 'utility'.

Price wished to restrict the word Picturesque to the sense which we have distinguished by a capital P, and to use it to describe the aesthetic pleasure which we receive from rough, shaggy and irregular scenes.[13] Knight disagreed with this restriction and believed that picturesque should be used to describe a scene which resembled a landscape painting.[14] Repton misunderstood his friends. He thought

122

The lake at Wingerworth, Derbyshire, was designed by Repton as 'an object of beauty' to be 'so managed as to admit of being occasionally drawn down two or three feet to supply canals, and other circumstances of advantage, in this populous and commercial part of the kingdom; exclusive of the increased supply of fish, where such food is in constant requisition'. Courtesy The British Library.

that Price advocated the Picturesque in preference to the Sublime and the Beautiful,[15] and that Knight advocated the picturesque in disregard of utility.[16]

Neither charge is substantiated by a close reading of Price and Knight — but it is easy to see how the mistakes arose. Price does concentrate on the Picturesque and Knight has very little to say about utility. Price's reason for giving more attention to the Picturesque was that earlier writers, especially Burke, had given it insufficient attention. He insisted he was 'by no means bigoted to the Picturesque or insensible to the charms of Beauty'.[17] His favourite instance of the Picturesque was a river with rocky banks, overhanging trees, rushing water and reedy swamps.

The difference between the three squires over utility also arose because Repton misunderstood his friends' books. Repton thought that Price's *Essay* of 1794 had advocated a wild, rugged and Picturesque area near the house, and that this idea was preposterous. When Price wrote in favour of terraces in his 1795 *Letter*,[18]

Price's estate at Foxley, Herefordshire, lay in an attractive valley. Today this has been marred by ill-considered poplar planting.

Repton declared the dispute settled. Price's remarks, he wrote, 'left no room for further controversy'.[19]

Repton criticised Knight for disregarding utility in his advocacy of the picturesque. In fact Knight's position was close to Burke's: he believed that utility and aesthetic pleasure are both good things but unconnected. Of the qualities which a herdsman and a poet see in a field of grass, Knight asks 'who shall presume to decide that the one are more truly and properly beauties than the other?'[20] His dispute with Repton was over what to say, not over what to do. They agreed that there should be a terrace between the house and the fields. Indeed Price tells us that the owner of Powis Castle was persuaded by Knight not to destroy the great terraces (p.122) which step down the hillside in front of the castle.[21]

Repton did not see an estate's profitability as the primary objective of his work. He aimed to produce 'a harmony of parts to the whole' and lamented the fact that he often had to 'contend with the opposition of stewards, the presumption and ignorance of gardeners and the jealousy of architects and builders'.[22] To accept that profit rather than harmony was his objective would have been to give way to one or other interested party. For this reason Repton preferred to see profit as a 'collateral prop'[23] for his views. When beauty and profit did coincide he was delighted. For example, the lake which he designed at Wingerworth (p.123) was beautiful and was planned to supply a canal with water and his client's table with fish.[24] Repton also liked the idea of a belt of copse woodland which could provide pleasant walks, shelter the corn, protect the cattle, supply cover for game, and provide the framework for his landscape design. He was, however, sorry to note that 'pecuniary advantage and ornament are seldom strictly compatible',[25] and he criticised Shenstone's *ferme ornée* for failing to unite ornament with profit.

Repton, Price and Knight each put the transition theory into practice. Little is known of Price's design for his own estate at Foxley (p.123). The foundations of the house and of what appears to have been a terraced garden can be detected, but the estate has been ruined by planting up the open spaces with poplars. Knight's estate at Downton (pp. 88, 89 and 129) remains in excellent condition and is one of the most romantic estates in England. In 1806 Repton wrote that Downton provided 'consummate proof' of Knight's good taste, but that 'it is impossible by description to convey an idea of its natural charms, or to do justice to that taste which has displayed these charms to the greatest advantage'.[26] Its very completeness as a work of art invites comparison with Rousham, Stourhead and Prior Park. Knight appears to have laid out the park wholly in the Irregular Style during his youth and to have converted it to the Transition Style by adding a neat terrace and a modest serpentine park. Comfort and convenience assume greater importance in middle age.

Repton lived in a cottage and treated the garden as the foreground to a Picturesque view of the village of Hare Street, Hertfordshire. There was even an irregular woodland on the hill in the background. The Transition Style also formed the basis of Repton's extensive practice. He was most unfortunate in that the prime years of his professional career, between the publication of his first book in 1795 and the collapse of his health in 1815, coincided with the Napoleonic Wars. The number and geographical extent of his commissions were

View from Repton's cottage in Hare Street — a small scale example of a transition from a Beautiful foreground, to a Picturesque village, to a wooded hill.

Repton's design for Sheringham Park, Norfolk. The North Sea provides a Sublime background, but the house in the Beautiful foreground (p.129) is sheltered from the wind.

The Reptons' design for the house at Sheringham, showing the foreground terrace.

The Transition Style in 1900 by T.H. Mawson. He wrote that 'any artist when painting a landscape, fills in, leaves out, or alters details, until he obtains his ideally balanced picture showing nature as he conceives it ought to be...the gardener wishes to recompose the landscape itself, and this mainly by the help of trees'. The transition runs from terrace to park to hills.

extraordinary for a country involved in a major European war, but the scope of the work his clients wished to have executed was modest by peacetime standards. Repton was highly skilled in the design of forests, parks and lakes, but in most cases his clients employed him to do little more than enrich the foreground of an existing scene with a garden.[27]

Once the fashion for sweeping agricultural land up to the living room windows had passed, there was a considerable demand for a cheerful 'dressed' area near the house. At Ashridge, which Repton considered one of his major works, a Beautiful foreground was added to a park designed by Brown. At Sheringham (pp.125 and 129) Repton had a rare opportunity to lay out a completely new estate, though a modest one by Brown's standards. Repton also designed the house with the help of his son and preferred this project 'over every other in which I have been consulted'.[28] The foreground at Sheringham is occupied by a small

A nineteenth century transition from house to pond to lawn at Biddulph Grange. The transition was included as one element in the Mixed Style.

A transition from art to nature at Polesden Lacey, Surrey, 1906-42.

terrace garden which is separated from the park by one of Repton's favourite devices, the balustrade. The middleground is most interesting: a straightforward serpentine park which might have been designed by Brown. The North Sea forms a Sublime background to the park but cannot be seen from the house. Repton would have liked it to be visible but he was dissuaded by climatic considerations from choosing a site in full exposure to the north wind. The North Sea, he observed, 'is not like that of the Bay of Naples'.[29]

The best account of the way in which nineteenth century designers interpreted the transition idea is to be found in Charles M'Intosh's *Book of the Garden*:

> Sir Uvedale Price clearly recognises a threefold division of the domain, which we have already referred to — namely, the architectural terrace and flower-garden, in direct connection with the house, where he admits the formal style; the shrubbery or pleasure-ground, a transition between the flowers and the trees, 'which we would hand over', says the writer [Sir Walter Scott] in the *Quarterly Review* already quoted, 'to the natural style of Brown and his school'; and thirdly, the park, which he considers the proper domain of his own system.[30]

The sketches by Mawson (p.126)[31] show how this idea was interpreted at the end of the century, but by this time it had become involved with the Italian Style.

Repton designed the terrace at Burley-on-the-Hill, Leicestershire, as the first stage of a transition. He proposed the reintroduction of terraces to English gardens to effect a smooth transition from house to garden, and from garden to park.   Courtesy Patrick Goode.

Left, Downton Castle, Shropshire, Richard Payne Knight's estate, provided 'consummate proof' of his good taste. Knight apparently laid out the park in the Irregular Style while a young man, but effectively converted it to the Transition Style by adding a terrace and serpentine park later in life.

Right, the Transition Style formed the basis of Repton's extensive practice, and at Sheringham, Norfolk, he had the rare opportunity to lay out a completely new estate, as well as design the house itself with help from his son.

Lambton Castle, Durham, forms part of a fine Italian scene which was created in the 1820s. Bonomi designed the castle.

An engraving of Isola Bella from Loudon's Encyclopaedia of Gardening. *Loudon agreed with James Wilson's description of the island as a 'miracle of artificial beauty'.*

The Italian Style

Repton's simple balustrades were sometimes adorned with urns and can be described as 'Italianate', but he was far from designing full-blown Italian gardens with flights of steps, statuary, fountains and terraces aligned round a central axis. Like all eighteenth century garden designers, Repton, Price and Knight were more interested in the landscape of antiquity than in Renaissance gardens.

The first nineteenth century author to praise the style of Italian and French Renaissance gardens was J.C. Loudon.[32] His admiration for what he called the 'ancient or geometrical style' was based on both observation and theory. In 1813, at the age of thirty, he sold his *ferme ornée* for a magnificent profit and set off to tour Europe. His admiration for the old formal gardens on the Continent grew during a number of tours between 1813 and 1819, and his opinion of English gardens was correspondingly diminished. In the first edition of his monumental *Encyclopaedia of Gardening* Loudon wrote:

> To say that landscape gardening is an improvement on geometric gardening is a similar misapplication of language as to say that a lawn is an improvement of a cornfield, because it is substituted in its place. It is absurd, therefore, to despise the ancient style...It has beauties of a different kind, equally perfect in their kind.[33]

He added that English landscape gardening 'can seldom succeed in producing anything higher than picturesque beauty'.

Loudon drew support for his unpatriotic views from the French Neoplatonic philosopher Quatremère de Quincy, whose *Essay on The Nature, The End and The Means of Imitation in the Fine Arts* was published in 1823. Quatremère was an art scholar, sculptor, antiquarian and encyclopaedist who believed that artists should imitate nature, and that 'nature' meant the Platonic world of ideas and forms. Quatremère criticised English gardens for not making use of the primary geometrical forms and for being more or less indistinguishable from raw nature:

> In fact, every element necessary to constitute imitation is absent [from irregular gardens]. Even the idea of repetition is scarcely traceable. What pretends to be an image of nature is nothing more or less than nature itself. The means of the art are reality. Everyone knows that the merit of its works consists in obviating any suspicion of art. To consitute a perfect garden, according to the irregular system of landscape gardening, we must not have the least suspicion that the grounds have been laid out by art.[34]

Loudon fully agreed and wrote that: 'forms perfectly regular, and divisions completely uniform, immediately excite the belief of design and, with this belief, all the admiration which follows the employment of skill'.[35]

Loudon's conversion to the Italian Style is one of the great turning points in the history of English garden design. He was the first theoretician to realise that the century-long quest to imitate ever-wilder versions of 'nature' had led into a dead end. When it was found that irregular gardens were indistinguishable from nature it became necessary to turn back and re-evaluate the traditional concern of the fine arts with abstract shapes and forms. Loudon's ill health persuaded him to withdraw from the practice of landscape design, but the designers who

Gardenesque planting at Sheffield Park, East Sussex. The aim was to display the characteristics of individual plants to their best advantage. J.C. Loudon, who invented the style, believed this would distinguish the planting as a work of art and enable people to learn more about botany.
Courtesy Marian Thompson

Joseph Paxton, who can be seen as a successor to Loudon, placed prehistoric monsters in the grounds of the Crystal Palace, Sydenham. These were not only Sublime features in a transition which ran from the terrace outside the glass palace, but also part of a geological and botanical display which served both educational and aesthetic objectives.

Underscar, in the Lake District, is one of the best surviving examples of Edward Kemp's work, and the garden adjoining the house is a fine example of the Mixed Style. Kemp used a distant view of Derwent Water and the Derwent Fells as the Sublime background to the garden scene.

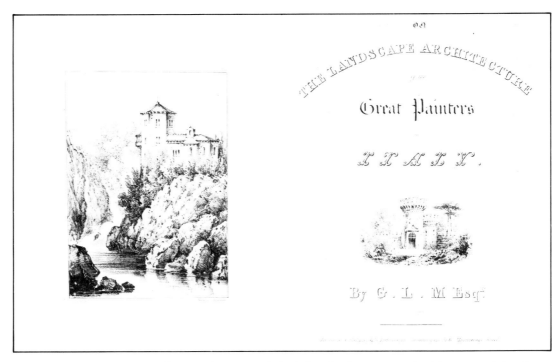

The title page of Gilbert Laing Meason's book On the Landscape Architecture of the Great Painters of Italy, *1828. This is the earliest use of the term 'landscape architecture'. The frontispiece shows a building from a painting by Dominichino.*　　Courtesy The British Library.

William Atkinson's design for Deepdene, one of the first nineteenth century Italian gardens.
Courtesy Lambeth Archives Department.

Deepdene, showing a transition from a balustraded terrace, through a serpentine park to a distant view.   Courtesy Lambeth Archives Department.

reintroduced the Italian Style to England during the nineteenth century were all familiar with his work and his writings.

One of the first designers to make full use of Italian garden ornament in England was the architect William Atkinson. He had done some architectural work at Scone Palace in 1803 when Loudon was working there on his irregular layout for the estate. In 1825 Atkinson was employed by Thomas Hope at Deepdene and Loudon praised his work as an example of 'landscape architecture' in the 1829 issue of the *Gardener's Magazine*.[36] Loudon's 1833 *Encyclopaedia of Cottage, Farm and Villa Architecture* gave further examples of 'landscape architecture' and Loudon observed that in modern Italian villas 'The regularity of the garden is, as it were, an accompanying decoration and support to the Architecture. The Architecture, sculpture, and gardens of these villas are often designed by the same hand, and concur in the general effect to produce perfect harmony'.[37] The term 'landscape architecture' had been coined by G.L. Meason in 1828 to describe a style of building which could be found in Italian landscape paintings.[38] This was its first use in relation to garden design. The garden at Deepdene had terraces at different levels, balustrades, flights of steps, repeated urns, alcoves and sculpture but no central axis. Hope had written an essay on gardens in 1808 which reveals him as an enthusiastic supporter of the Transition Style,[39] and the Italian garden at Deepdene was the first stage in a transition which ran through the park and over the lake to a distant view of Box Hill.

Most of the Italian gardens which were made in Victorian England were conceived as the first stage in a transition. Charles Barry, who was a contributor to Loudon's *Architectural Magazine,* designed his first Italian terrace at Trentham

GARDEN IN GEOMETRIC STYLE.

William Blackwood & Sons

The art of floral bedding, or mosaiculture, has virtually vanished from private gardens but survives in public parks and institutional gardens. The fine example above is at Cannizaro in south west London; opposite top, a reconstructed Victorian bedding scheme at the Bowes Museum, Barnard Castle.

Opposite left, a design for geometrical bedding by Charles M'Intosh (from The Book of the Garden, *1853) who worked for the Duke of Buccleuch at Dalkeith Palace and for the King of the Belgians at Claremont. Many patterns of this type were published in books and journals and gardeners competed to produce schemes which would delight their employers and excite the admiration of friends.*
Courtesy The British Library.

The Italian Terrace at Harewood House is the first stage in a transition.

Charles Barry's Italian terrace at Trentham. It provided a foreground for a park designed by Lancelot Brown.

in 1834, one year after the publication of Loudon's encyclopaedia. Trentham appears to have set a fashion for adding Italian terraces to Brownian parks, and Barry was commissioned to design similar terraces at Holkham, Cliveden and Harewood. Barry also designed the Italian terrace in Trafalgar Square. W.A. Nesfield, who worked at Trentham with Barry, was responsible for a number of Italian terraces. Most of them have disappeared, but the terrace in front of the plant house at Kew Gardens and the parterre on the south side of Castle Howard are well maintained. In 1848 Barry designed an Italian garden at Shrubland, Suffolk, which has a full axial layout (p.142). It was a significant departure from the Transition Style.

Joseph Paxton was an enthusiast for the Italian Style and the man who most completely adopted 'Loudon's mantle'. He made his first lake at the age of nineteen, in the year which saw the publication of Loudon's *Encyclopaedia of Gardening*. It had a chapter on the 'Education of Gardeners' which contained the following advice for young gardeners:

> Suppose, for example, a man desires to be a king; that is a desire sufficiently extraordinary; but if he will first make himself acquainted with the history of men who have raised themselves from nothing to be kings...he may very likely attain his object...Let no young gardener, therefore, who reads this, even if he can but barely read, imagine that he

Alton Towers, Staffordshire, is the best surviving example of the Mixed Style. It was fully described by Loudon in the 1830s (pp.155-157 and 159), though he did not consider it a model to be imitated. Such gardens have considerable appeal, and Alton Towers is in danger of being swamped by an amusement park.

Elements of the Mixed Style can be seen, opposite, at Sezincote, Gloucestershire — the Indian garden, and, opposite top, at Brighton Pavilion, East Sussex (with floral bedding in evidence). The Pavilion grounds were based on a design by Repton who should be seen as the inventor of the Mixed Style and whose last book contained proposals for a variety of 'different kinds of gardens'.

141

At Shrubland, Suffolk, Barry designed an Italian garden with an axial layout.
Courtesy The British Library.

may not become eminent in any of the pursuits of life...to desire and apply is to attain, and the attainment will be in proportion to the application.[40]

Four years later Paxton was appointed head gardener to the Duke of Devonshire at Chatsworth and Loudon began publication of his *Gardener's Magazine*. The magazine contained voluminous advice on self-education for gardeners and Paxton absorbed it all. He worked with Jeffry Wyatville on the Italian gardens at Chatsworth, which divide the house from the Brownian park, and in 1831 he started a horticultural periodical to rival Loudon's. In 1850 he used Loudon's method of greenhouse construction to build the Crystal Palace, and the following year he set up a company which spent £1.2m on moving the Palace to Sydenham and installing it in a magnificent Italian garden. This was as near as an apprentice gardener from a poor home could get to becoming a king in Victorian England. The waterworks at Sydenham were intended to outshine Versailles and wide terraces stepped down the hill on both sides of a long central axis. However, Paxton was not able to resist the transition idea completely. He included an irregular lake at the far end of the axis and one of the most Sublime features in any English garden: a romantic island inhabited by models of prehistoric monsters (p.132). Paxton also employed the Italian Style for the grounds at Mentmore and the People's Park in Halifax[41] (p.145).

The style was very popular in nineteenth century public parks. It is shown in the drawing as an axial terraced garden which has been added to an existing park.

The Italian Style in England: a series of terraces organised on a central axis and often set in an existing park.

The remains of Paxton's most magnificent terraces at the Crystal Palace, London.

143

Mixed Style garden designs, left, at Winterbourne, Birmingham — the Chinese bridge and, below, at Tatton Park, Cheshire — The Japanese garden. Mixed Style gardens were symbolic of the Victorian thirst for travel and spiritual adventure.

The People's Park, Halifax, designed by Joseph Paxton. It has an Italian Style terrace and a central axis leading to dense Victorian planting.

The Italian garden at Bowood, Wiltshire, was designed by George Kennedy and added to Brown's park there in the 1860s.

The Italian garden at the head of the Serpentine, Hyde Park, London, was designed in 1861 by John Thomas.

146

Victorian planting design

The aesthetic considerations which led Loudon to praise Italian gardens also led him to devise a style of planting design which he named the 'gardenesque'.[42] Loudon believed that there were two ways of evading the anomaly of making 'gardens' which could not be distinguished from 'nature'. The first was to base their layout on abstract shapes. The second was to make exclusive use of plants which are not native to the area in which the garden was made, and to keep the plants well separated from each other so that they can be recognised as exotics (p.132). This is the intellectual origin of the specimen trees and shrubs which are still dotted around in English gardens.

Loudon described the main idea behind the gardenesque style of planting as the 'Principle of Recognition' and asserted that 'Any creation, to be recognised as a work of art, must be such as can never be mistaken for a work of nature'.[43] His rules for applying the principle to landscape gardening were of the utmost rigour:

Gardenesque planting in Birmingham Botanical Garden. Loudon designed the garden in 1831.

> The gardenesque is found exclusively in single trees, which have been planted in favourable situations; not pressed on during their growth, by any other objects; and allowed to throw out their branches equally on every side, uninjured by cattle or other animals; and, if touched by the hand of the gardener, only to be improved in their regularity and symmetry.[44]
>
> The brook, lake, or river, is readily appropriated as a work of art, by planting exotic, woody, and herbaceous plants along the margins, in a natural-looking manner; carefully removing all that are indigenous.[45]
>
> Even the turf should be composed of grasses different from those of the surrounding grass fields.[46]

Loudon also discussed the problem of making a natural outcrop of rocks at Piercefield (p.148) look artificial:

> By what means are the perpendicular rocks on the banks of the river Wye, at Piercefield in Monmouthshire, to be rendered a work of art? By substituting another kind of rock for the indigenous one? No; for not only is the scale too large to render this practicable, but, if it were accomplished, the very largeness of the scale would make it be still considered as the work of nature; unless, indeed, rocks, which every one knew did not exist in the country at all, were substituted for the natural ones.[47]

His solution was to remove all the indigenous vegetation and replace it with 'foreign vegetation of a similar character'. Given the absurd impracticality of such

147

Above, gardenesque planting at Wakehurst Place, West Sussex. The estate is run by the Royal Botanic Gardens, Kew, and the plants are both well grown and well labelled.

Below left, the perpendicular rocks at Piercefield in the Wye Valley. Loudon discussed the means by which they could be transformed into a recognisable 'work of art' (p.147).
Courtesy Marian Thompson.

Below right, the Derby Arboretum, designed and planted by Loudon. He would be horrified to know that the parks department no longer names the specimen trees.

expedients it is no cause for wonder that Loudon preferred regular gardens. However, he also liked to see exotic plants arranged in naturalistic groups — providing they were well grown and well labelled.

Loudon's passionate interest in the plants which made the gardenesque style possible brought his family close to financial ruin. His wife gave the following account:

> From the year 1833 to Midsummer 1838 Mr. Loudon underwent the most extraordinary exertions both of mind and body. Having resolved that all the drawings of trees for the *Arboretum* [see below] should be made from nature, he had seven artists constantly employed, and he was frequently in the open air with them from his breakfast at seven in the morning till he came home to dinner at eight in the evening, having remained the whole of that time without taking the slightest refreshment, and generally without even sitting down... In addition to the large sums in ready money he paid to the artists and other persons employed during the progress of the *Arboretum,* he found at its conclusion that he owed ten thousand pounds to the printer, the stationer, and the wood-engraver who had been employed on that work.[48]

Gardenesque planting at Leonardslee Gardens, West Sussex.

The *Arboretum et Fruiticetum Britannicum* was eventually published in eight volumes with 'upwards of 2,500 engravings'. Professor Sir Joseph Hooker wrote:

> There is not a naturalist in Europe who could have executed the task with anything like the talent, and judgement, and accuracy, that is here displayed by Mr. Loudon...In short, nothing is omitted, either in the descriptive or pictorial matter, which can tend to illustrate the history and uses of *trees* and *shrubs*...it will be seen at once of what vast importance must such a work be to this country, to every part of Europe, and the temperate parts of North America; and we may even say, to all the temperate parts of the civilised world.[49]

Loudon designed an excellent arboretum in Derby which survives in reasonable condition — though the parks department does not label the specimen plants.[50]

Hooker judged the importance of the *Arboretum* correctly. He became the first Director of Kew Gardens two years after reviewing the book and set about arranging the trees and shrubs in accordance with the principle which Loudon had

Repton's flower garden at Valleyfield, Fife. It is a precursor of the Victorian craze for floral bedding. Courtesy The British Library.

The carpet bedding at Hardwick Hall, Derbyshire, once displayed Elizabeth Shrewsbury's initials.

The garden at Hoole House, Cheshire, c.1837. Loudon praised 'the perfect unity of the circular beds'.

derived from Sir Uvedale Price. Hooker opened the gardens to the public. The exotic trees and shrubs at Kew are arranged in naturalistic groups and great attention is paid to botanical accuracy— though Hooker and his successors have not prevented plants from being 'pressed on during their growth'.[51] The same idea was employed by Paxton in the arboretum at Chatsworth and has been repeated in woodland gardens throughout the land. Some of the best examples of gardenesque planting are to be found at Wakehurst Place, Birmingham Botanical Garden (designed by Loudon), the Royal Botanic Garden in Edinburgh, Bodnant, Nymans, Sheffield Park (p.132) and Leonardslee. Woodland gardens of similar character can be found, as Hooker predicted, in 'all the temperate parts of the civilised world'. They can be classified as gardenesque if they are laid out with the emphasis on botanical display and as Picturesque or irregular if the emphasis is on pictorial effect.

Floral bedding, or mosaiculture, is the other famous Victorian style of planting design (pp.136 and 137). Its distant origins lie in the knots and parterres of Renaissance Europe. Its immediate origins can be found in the flower gardens designed by Humphry Repton at Valleyfield, Ashridge, Woburn and many of his other later projects. These were part of the plan for making Beautiful foregrounds as the first stage in the Transition Style. The patterns which were used bear a distinct resemblance to Victorian bedding patterns, but Repton does not say that they were stocked with tender plants and changed at regular intervals. The principle on which the 'changeable flower garden' was managed are explained in Loudon's 1822 *Enclycopaedia*:

> All the plants are kept in pots, and reared in a flower nursery or reserve
> ground. As soon as they begin to flower, they are plunged in the borders
> of the flower garden, and, whenever they show symptoms of decay,
> removed, to be replaced by others from the same source.[52]

In 1822 this practice was not so common as the 'mingled flower garden', in

Above, circular beds in Greenwich Park, London — an outstanding modern example of a favourite nineteenth century practice.

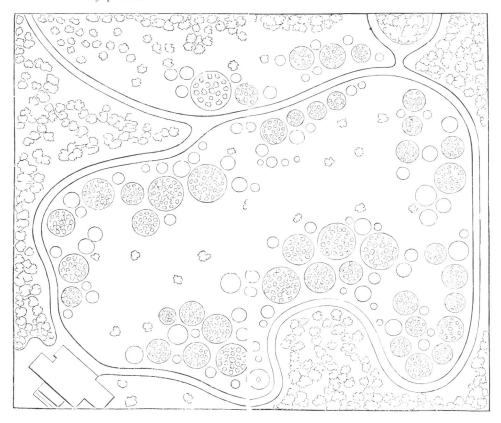

Circular beds designed by Edward Kemp at Stanley Park, Liverpool.

which flowers were mixed with shrubs, but in the 1840s floral bedding became a craze. Flower gardens took on the appearance of brightly coloured carpets and gardeners vied with each other to produce new and ever more dazzling displays.

Loudon preferred to see bedding plants in circular beds. He considered the circle to be the purest geometrical shape and also the most practical for flower beds of all kinds:

> We wish we could strongly impress in the mind of **every** amateur, and of every gardener, that, for all general purposes of planting beds of shrubs, or beds of flowers on a lawn...the best form is the circle, provided that it be always kept of small size, say from 18in. to 6ft. in diameter, one circle never placed nearer to another than 2ft., and these beds be thrown together in groups or constellations, as stars are in the firmament.[53]

Loudon's wish was granted. Almost a century and a half has passed since he wrote the above passage and the circular flower bed retains its popularity in suburban gardens and public parks — along with the star which has been brought down from the firmament and is also used as a shape for flower beds.

Joseph Paxton excelled at the art of floral bedding, and filled the grounds of Chatsworth, Mentmore and the Crystal Palace with the most elaborate displays. Geometric bedding was one of the chief attractions of the Crystal Palace and Paxton was most annoyed when publicly financed parks departments started making displays of bedding plants which could be viewed without paying an

Left, a design for circular flower beds by Loudon. He wrote that 'the simplicity of the circular form is a...point of beauty in itself, and...it is besides the most convenient form for culture'.

153

Victorian planting at Chillingham Castle, Northumberland, c.1900.

Floral bedding at Mentmore, Buckinghamshire, c.1900. Paxton designed both the house and gardens.

admission charge. Edward Kemp and Charles M'Intosh, who succeeded Loudon as popular writers on garden design, included patterns for bedding in their books (p.136) and whetted the public's appetite for new designs. M'Intosh even wrote a learned section on the application of the principles of colour harmony to the design of bedding schemes which contained references to Repton, Loudon, Newton and Chevreul (a famous writer on the theory of colour harmony).[54]

The Mixed Style

Garden historians like to say that Loudon invented the Mixed or Gardenesque Style and that Alton Towers, Staffordshire, is the best surviving example. Their reasoning appears to be that Alton Towers is described in the *Gardener's Magazine,* which Loudon edited, and that it looks like a physical counterpart to his encyclopaedias on gardening and architecture: a vast assemblage of plants and garden buildings in styles from all parts of the known world (pp.140, 156, 157 and 159). Alton Towers *is* the best example of the Mixed Style but it was severely criticised by Loudon and the planting design is hardly gardenesque. The plants are in irregular groups but the collection is of very marginal interest to plantsmen and there is no evidence of a botanical zest for identification, classification and variety. As an encyclopaedist, Loudon was appalled by the mixture of styles at Alton Towers. After visiting the place in 1826 and again in 1831 he wrote the following description of the gardens:

> Alton Towers is a very singular place, both in its geology, which is peculiarly adopted for grand and picturesque effects, and in what has been

The Mixed Style at Wimbledon House: an illustration from Loudon's Suburban Gardener.

Vases, stone stairs, fountains and rocks at Alton Towers, c.1834. This, and the other illustrations on this page are from Loudon's Encyclopaedia of Gardening.

A range of architectural conservatories and castellated stabling (see p.140).

A corkscrew fountain of 'a peculiar description'.

An imitation of Stonehenge.

The yew arches at Alton Towers in 1900.

done to it by the late Earl of Shrewsbury . . . This nobleman, abounding
in wealth, always fond of architecture and gardening, but with much more
fancy than sound judgement, seems to have wished to produce something
different from everything else. Though he consulted almost every artist,
ourselves among the rest, he seems only to have done so for the purpose
of avoiding whatever an artist might recommend. After passing in review
before him a great number of ideas, that which he adopted was always
different from everything that had been proposed to him.[55]

Loudon found the consequences of the Earl's policy very mixed indeed:

The first objects that met our eye were the dry Gothic bridge and the
embankment leading to it, with a huge imitation of Stonehenge beyond
and a pond above the level of the bridge alongside of it, backed by a mass
of castellated stabling. Farther along the side of the valley, to the left of
the bridge, is a range of architectural conservatories, with seven elegant
glass domes, designed by Mr. Abraham, richly gilt. Farther on, still to the
left, and placed on a high and bold naked rock, is a lofty Gothic tower or
temple . . . consisting of several tiers of balconies, round a central staircase
and rooms; the exterior ornaments numerous, and resplendent with
gilding. Near the base of the rock is a corkscrew fountain of a peculiar
description . . . below the main range of conservatories [is] a paved terrace
walk with a Grecian temple at one end . . . The remainder of the valley, to
the bottom, and on the opposite side, displays such a labyrinth of terraces,

157

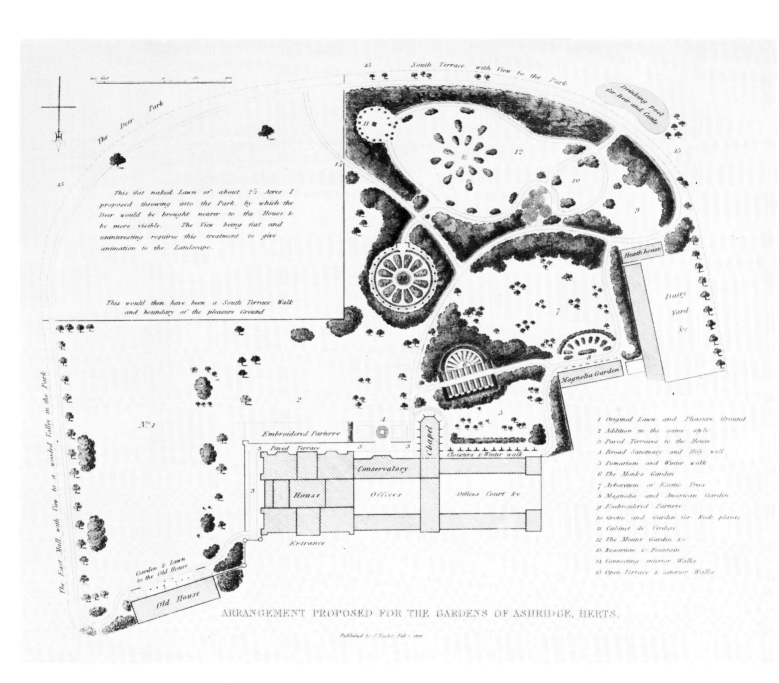

South Terrace with View to the Park

Drinking Pool for Deer and Cattle

The Deer Park

This flat naked Lawn of about 2½ Acres I proposed throwing into the Park by which the Deer would be brought nearer to the House & be more visible. The View being flat and uninteresting requires this treatment to give animation to the Landscape.

This would then have been a South Terrace Walk and boundary of the pleasure Ground

Heath house

Dairy Yard &c

Magnolia Garden

The East Walk with View to a wooded Valley in the Park

No 1

No 2

Embroidered Parterre

Paved Terrace

Chapel

Cloisters & Winter walk

Conservatory

House

Offices

Offices Court &c

Entrance

Garden & Lawn to the Old House

Old House

1 Original Lawn and Pleasure Ground
2 Addition in the same style
3 Paved Terraces to the House
4 Broad Sanctuary and Holy well
5 Pomarium and Winter walk
6 The Monk's Garden
7 Arboretum or Exotic Trees
8 Magnolia and American Garden
9 Embroidered Parterre
10 Grotto and Garden for Rock plants
11 Cabinet de Verdure
12 The Mount Garden &c
13 Rosarium & Fountain
14 Connecting interior Walks
15 Open Terrace & exterior Walks

ARRANGEMENT PROPOSED FOR THE GARDENS OF ASHRIDGE, HERTS.

Published by J Taylor Feb 1 1816

The origin of the Mixed Style — Humphry Repton's collection of 'gardens of different styles, dates, characters and dimensions' at Ashridge, Hertfordshire. Repton believed that collecting gardens in different styles was rather like collecting books or paintings. Courtesy The British Library.

curious architectural walls, trellis-work arbours, vases, statues, stone stairs, wooden stairs, turf stairs, pavements, gravel and grass walks, ornamental buildings, bridges, porticoes, temples, pagodas, gates, iron railings, parterres, jets, ponds, streams, seats, fountains, caves, flower baskets, waterfalls, rocks, cottages, trees, shrubs, beds of flowers, ivied walls, rockwork, shellwork, rootwork, moss houses, old trunks of trees, entire dead trees, &c., that it is utterly impossible for words to give any idea of the effect...in one place we have Indian temples excavated in it, covered with hieroglyphics; and in another, a projecting rock is formed into a huge serpent, with a spear-shaped iron tongue and glass eyes.[56]

It is difficult to conceive of a garden with a greater mixture of stylistic features than Alton Towers. Loudon most certainly did not consider it a model to be imitated, and concluded: 'We consider the greater part of it in excessively bad taste, or rather, perhaps, as the work of a morbid imagination, joined to the command of unlimited resources'.[57]

Alton Towers is now a popular amusement park which attracts large crowds. It is known as a theme park. The more ephemeral garden features have gone, but the main garden structures were soundly built and are well maintained. Time and the Earl's lavish plantings have welded them into a unified whole which has the self-confident exuberance of the great nineteenth century railway stations, piers, hotels and churches. Like these buildings, the gardens at Alton Towers can be seen as symbols of the nineteenth century thirst for travel, comfort and spiritual adventure.

The real inventor of the Mixed Style was Humphry Repton. His last book contains proposals for a variety of 'different kinds of gardens', which were restrained by the standard of Alton Towers but very mixed by the refined standards of the eighteenth century. Repton described Ashridge as 'the child of my age and declining powers' and his 'youngest favourite', adding that few other projects had 'excited so much interest in my mind'.[58] He published a fragment from the Ashridge Red Book in which he justified the mixture of features as follows:

> The novelty of this attempt to collect a number of gardens, differing from each other, may perhaps, excite the critic's censure; but I will hope there is no more absurdity in collecting gardens of different styles, dates, characters, and dimensions, in the same enclosure, than in placing the works of a Raphael and a Teniers in the same cabinet, or books sacred and profane in the same library.[59]

Repton's powers may have been declining, but his reasoning had a most potent effect on Victorian gardens. The Ashridge Red Book proposed no less than fifteen different types of garden. They included a holy well in an enclosure of rich masonry, a winter garden, a monks' garden (p.160), a sheltered garden for foreign trees, an American garden, raised beds, and a rosarium (p.161), which was 'supplied from the holy well, and then led into the grotto, from whence it is finally conducted into the drinking-pool in the park'. The succeeding fragment from the Red Book on Woburn Abbey proposed another American garden and a Chinese-dairy 'decorated by an assemblage of Chinese plants, such as the Hydrangea,

Repton's design for the monks' garden at Ashridge, Hertford-shire.

The monks' garden at Ashridge, c.1900.

Repton's design for the rosarium at Ashridge.

A Reptonian rosarium at Belton House, Lincolnshire, c.1900.

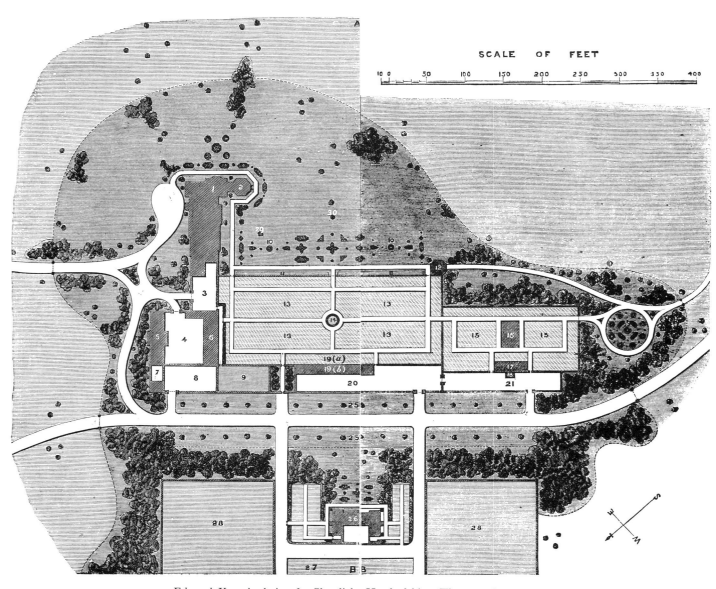

Edward Kemp's design for Shendish, Hertfordshire. The area shown on this plan is part of a larger garden in the Mixed Style.

Aucuba, and Camellia japonica'.[60] Since Repton's *Fragments on the Theory and Practice of Landscape Gardening* was published in 1816, and Alton Towers was made between 1814 and 1827, it seems likely that Repton, as the most famous landscape designer and gardening author of his day, was the predominant influence on the Earl of Shrewsbury. However, Repton's different types of garden were only intended to make the foreground more Beautiful; the Earl and many subsequent designers applied the style to whole estates.

Edward Kemp published the first edition of his highly successful book on garden design, *How to Lay Out a Small Garden,* in 1850 and included a number of Reptonesque designs by his own hand. It is perhaps the most representative of all Victorian books on garden design.

Kemp advocated 'the mixed style, with a little help from both the formal and the picturesque' and, fearing that this might not be a sufficient mixture, he went on to say that 'an absolute adherence to one style is not, therefore, to be reckoned among the paramount virtues of the art', and

The garden at Shendish where some of Kemp's plantings are still in existence. The building is marked 12 on the plan opposite.

Part of the mixed garden at Underscar, in the Lake District, designed by Edward Kemp (p.133).

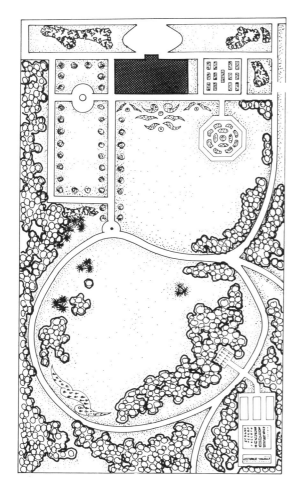

The Mixed Style: a variety of features and types of gardens, assembled like works of art in a gallery, or books in a library.

even individual styles should be adapted to fit in with the peculiarities of individual sites (pp. 133, 162 and 163).[61]

Believers in stylistic purity may never appreciate the Mixed Style but its popular appeal has always been great. Surprisingly few good examples remain, though several survive within thirty miles of Alton Towers: Biddulph Grange, Tatton Park and Shugborough. In order to gain a full appreciation of the style it is necessary to resort to one of three expedients: one can look at contemporary illustrations (especially Loudon's); one can look at the photographic books which were published between 1890 and 1914; or one can go on tour and set the remembered images beside each

The Egyptian garden at Biddulph Grange, Staffordshire, in the early years of this century.

The Great Conservatory at Sefton Park, Liverpool.

other in one's mind. The tour could well start with a visit to the surviving parts of Repton's work at Woburn and Ashridge. It should then include the following:

* Alton Towers
* the aviary at Waddesdon Manor
* the aboretum at Chatsworth
* the circular rosary at Regent's Park
* the Indian garden at Sezincote (p.141)
* the Italian terrace and the rose gardens at Shugborough
* the Brighton Pavilion, based on a Repton design (p.141)
* the Chinese and Egyptian gardens at Biddulph Grange
* the alpine garden in the Edinburgh Royal Botanic Garden
* the bamboo glade and the Palm House at Kew Gardens
* the Great Conservatory in Sefton Park
* the conservatory and the American garden at Bicton
* the Swiss Cottage at Osborne
* the Japanese garden and the fernery at Tatton Park (p.144)
* the Chinese bridge at Winterbourne, Birmingham (p.144)
* the prehistoric monsters at the Crystal Palace (p.132)

The variety of countries in the above list remind us that the Mixed Style helped to satisfy the nineteenth century globe-trottting Englishman's taste for the exotic. Nowadays he turns to the television set, the package tour and the *National Geographic Magazine*.

CHAPTER V

1870-1985 : *The Arts and Crafts and Abstract Styles; Recent Trends*

The Arts and Crafts Style

The principle that gardens should imitate nature slumbered during the middle years of the nineteenth century. Loudon's discussion of the subject merely confused his successors. They paid their respects to the theory but gave no active consideration to the question of *how* gardens should be made to imitate nature. Edward Kemp's attitude is representative:

> Readers who have travelled with me thus far will have perceived that I have had occasion more than once to refer to Nature as the great school of landscape gardening. It may be worth while, then, specifically to inquire how far the *imitation of nature* is possible and right. I profess not to be of those who would carry this principle very far, or into minor matters...A garden is for comfort, and convenience, and luxury, and use, as well as for making a beautiful picture. It is to express civilisation, and care, and design, and refinement...In these respects, it is fundamentally different from all natural scenes.[1]

So it was that Dame Nature slept. In the 1870s a prince came forward to awaken the sleeping beauty. His name was William Robinson.

Robinson was twenty-nine in 1867 and spent that summer touring the parks

Subtropical planting. Robinson admired the bold foliage of palms and tree ferns, but thought the cost unnecessary.

Bold foliage effects with hardy plants: the frontispiece to Robinson's Wild Garden, *engraved by Alfred Parsons in 1880.*

and gardens of France as a correspondent for *The Gardener's Chronicle.* The weather was bad and English correspondents complained about the way in which their floral bedding schemes were being ruined by 'cold nipping winds...followed almost continuously by cold nights, and an unusually heavy rainfall'.[2] Various suggestions were submitted for breeding tougher plants, for using foliage plants which would not decay in bad weather, and for using new patterns of circles and stars to delight the eye and ensure that 'our employers will inspect their neighbour's floral decorations again with pleasure'.[3]

One solution to the problem was developed in Paris. Monsieur Barillet-Deschamps experimented with palms, tree ferns and other subtropical plants which were less affected by the weather and did not depend on flowers for effect. The foliage plants were also used in more natural groups than floral bedding. Robinson was impressed, though he noted that practical men were saying 'This subtropical system will never do for England'.[4]

John Gibson tried out the system in Battersea Park during 1867. It was popular but expensive. Robinson gave a further account of the subtropical system in his *Gleanings from French Gardens,* and said that equally natural effects could be obtained by using hardy plants: 'We have no doubt whatsoever that in many places as good an effect as any yet seen in an English garden from tender plants may be obtained by planting hardy ones only![5] He particularly recommended the use of pampas grass (opposite and p.180), yuccas, bamboos, crambe and rheum. As he later wrote in the *Wild Garden*: 'I was led to think of the enormous number of beautiful hardy plants from other countries which might be naturalised with a very slight amount of trouble'.[6] Thus was an old style revived by the English weather, nature and economy.

Robinson became a militant protagonist of naturalistic planting (p.177) and an opponent of floral bedding. He was equally opposed to the use of tender flowering plants and to their arrangement in geometrical beds, especially in even-height 'carpet' beds (p.150). His beliefs constituted an unwitting return to the principles of planting design which had been formulated by Sir Uvedale Price. When Christopher Hussey remarked upon the ancestry of Robinson's wild planting, he was summoned to Gravetye Manor where Robinson told him that he had 'never heard' of Sir Uvedale Price.[7] Robinson saw Loudon as his great predecessor and devoted a series of articles to him in the first issues of his own periodical *The Garden*. This was partly true: Loudon followed Price in liking natural groups of plants, providing they were well grown and well labelled. The point which Robinson missed or ignored is that Loudon's Neoplatonic conception of nature also led him to recommend geometrical flower beds. As M'Intosh noted: 'Circular figures. . .in laying out flower gardens' were 'strongly advocated by the late Mr. Loudon'.[8]

Robinson's attack on floral and carpet bedding was in tune with current artistic and scientific ideas and, as a result, it attracted widespread support in Victorian England. Robinson became friends with John Ruskin and found him an energetic ally in Nature's cause. At the age of twenty Ruskin had, in fact, already written for the *Architectural Magazine,* and Loudon, forthright as ever in his judgement, welcomed him as 'the greatest natural genius that it has ever been my fortune to become acquainted with'.[9] At the age of thirty Ruskin published the *Seven Lamps of Architecture* and identified nature as one of the main sources of beauty:

> I do not mean to assert that every happy arrangement of line is directly suggested by a natural object; but that all beautiful lines are adaptations of those which are commonest in the external creation. . .The pointed arch is beautiful; it is the termination of every leaf that shakes in summer wind, and its most fortunate associations are directly borrowed from the trefoiled grass of the field, or from the stars of its flowers.[10]

Robinson was delighted to have such a powerful authority behind him and never tired of reiterating the dependence of art upon Nature with a capital N: 'The work of the artist is always marked by its fidelity to Nature'.[11] It was a restatement of one of the principles of the arts and crafts movement. William Morris was sympathetic to Robinson's point of view and wrote:

> Another thing also too commonly seen is an aberration of the human mind, which otherwise I should have been ashamed to warn you of. It is technically called carpet bedding. Need I explain further? I had rather not, for when I think of it even when I am quite alone I blush with shame at the thought.[12]

When Robinson found his attack on bedding had become a popular cause, his confidence grew and he criticised the use of all straight lines in gardens. This led

Pampas grass used instead of subtropical plants. An illustration from Robinson's English Flower Garden.

A young lady sketching at Kenwood, from Loudon's Suburban Gardener, *1838. Loudon believed that 'the improvement which, within the last fifty years, has taken place in landscape gardening, is, in a great measure, owing to the more general adoption of the art of sketching landscapes from nature, as a branch of female education'.*

him to oppose the use of terraces and architectural features as vigorously as Brown's supporters had done in the second half of the eighteenth century. His enthusiasm for wildness and romance reached such a pitch that he came near to advocating the Irregular Style.

Although Robinson's views on geometric bedding were supported by arts and crafts architects, his views on terraces and other architectural features were not. Reginald Blomfield and J.D. Sedding, both architects and members of the Art Workers' Guild, wrote books on garden design and advocated terraces.[13] [14] Sedding was comparatively moderate, but a furious dispute arose between Robinson and Blomfield as to whether or not gardens should have terraces. Robinson had gone too far in opposing terraces and Blomfield went too far in opposing Robinson. Blomfield insisted that there must be no natural shapes or planting anywhere near the house. It was a most surprising recurrence of an argument which had been effectively settled in the 1790s by Repton and the introduction of the Transition Style. In the 1890s the mediator who stepped in to settle the dispute was a person destined to fulfil Loudon's prediction that nothing was likely to have such a good effect on the art of garden design as the fact that so many young ladies were taking up landscape painting.[15]

Gertrude Jekyll was born in 1843, the year in which Loudon died. When young she had studied painting at the Kensington School of Art and became an admirer, and later friend, of John Ruskin. Her whole approach to life and work was based on the arts and crafts movement. Had the Art Workers' Guild permitted lady members she would doubtless have joined and might have restrained Blomfield at an earlier date. Jekyll was skilled at numerous arts and practised each with a loving care for craftsmanship, naturalness and beauty. One of her arts was

THE TERRACE : HADDON HALL : DERBYSHIRE

Above, Robinson's engraving of Haddon Hall, Derbyshire, from his book The English Flower Garden, *emphasises the growth of hardy plants on the walls and balustrades. Left, Bloomfield's engraving of Haddon Hall, from his book* The Formal Garden in England, *emphasises the formal terraces near the house.*

Robinson's terrace garden at Gravetye Manor, West Sussex, from The English Flower Garden. *It is surprisingly geometrical for a garden designed by an advocate of wild gardening.*

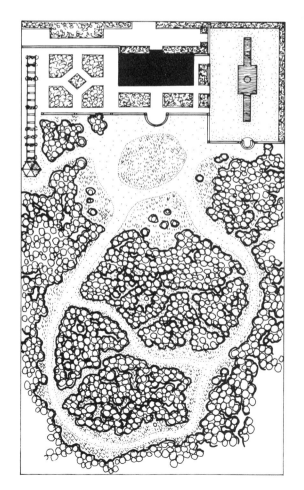

gardening and, with Robinson's help, she began to contribute to the horticultural press. Jekyll wrote with great authority and became a highly respected figure in the gardening world.

In 1896 she considered the arguments which had been advanced by Robinson and Blomfield and pronounced judgement: 'Both are right, both are wrong'. You could, Jekyll believed, have a terrace near the house, but you should arrange your plants in natural groups. She thought both the disputants hot headed, but was somewhat more inclined to Robinson's side, and added the comment that Blomfield seemed to be saying 'there is no garden but the formal garden...and I am his prophet!'[16] Blomfield accepted her judgement and, in the third edition of his book, sheepishly referred to 'a somewhat acrid controversy' between landscape gardeners and architects in which 'there was a good deal of truth on both sides'.[17] Robinson bought an estate in Sussex which needed a terrace, and Blomfield an estate on the island of Jersey which lent itself to the design of a wild garden.

In plan terms the dispute was resolved by an updated version of the Transition Style. The contestants agreed that the ideal arrangement was to have a broad walk or a terrace near the house, and then a transition, first to an open lawn and then beyond to a woodland garden or a fine view. The three elements of this sequence are shown in the drawing. It represents a garden of about five hectares. Jekyll considered this to be 'small'. Her own garden was less than seven hectares in extent and she could

The Arts and Crafts Style: a transition from a terrace to a woodland garden, with vernacular detailing and planting in the Irregular Style.

Above, Gertrude Jekyll's design for a terraced garden, with rills of water as at the Villa d'Este, and, right, a rill of the type which Gertrude Jekyll admired at the Villa d'Este outside Rome.

manage it with the help of eleven men. Few property agents would consider seven hectares unduly small, but even one hundred and seven hectares would have been tiny for one of the old estates for which the Transition Style was developed.

Since Repton was the chief professional advocate of the transition it is worth noting that Jekyll and Sedding both praise him. Jekyll wrote that Repton teaches us 'to see how to join house to garden and garden to woodland';[18] Sedding that 'the best advice you can give to a young gardener is — know your Repton'.[19]

Jekyll became the most powerful influence on the revival of English garden design at the turn of the century. Her own taste for terraces probably dated from her youthful tours of Italy and the Mediterranean. Her second book, *Wall and Water Gardens,* contains photographs of the Villa d'Este and a plan for 'one small section' of a garden which 'I have ventured to describe and figure in detail'.[20] Her design was for an elaborate terraced garden with rills of water running down both sides of a flight of steps in the Italian manner. The geometry of Italian gardens, then as now, was softened by a profusion of evergreen plants. The delightful combination of straight and irregular lines attracted Jekyll's eye and became a feature of the Arts and Crafts Style. An indication of how it was interpreted in an English context with different vernacular traditions can be gained by placing Robinson and Blomfield's illustrations alongside one another. In the illustrations overleaf Blomfield's show the types of space which characterised the style and Robinson's the vocabulary of hardy plants in natural groupings which were used to adorn the spaces.

GARDEN AND TERRACE : MONTACUTE : SOMERSET :

Above, the garden and terrace at Montacute, from Blomfield's The Formal Garden in England. *Right, a small child amongst hardy plants, from Robinson's* The English Flower Garden. *Below, The old garden at Brickwall, from Blomfield's* The Formal Garden in England.

The illustrations on this and the facing page show the enclosed spaces which characterise the Arts and Crafts Style, and the type of planting which was used to adorn the spaces.

THE OLD GARDENS AT BRICKWALL NEAR NORTHIAM : SUSSEX

'*A colony of myrrhis odorata, established in a shrubbery with harebells here and there*'. *The quote and the illustration are from Robinson's* The Wild Garden.

A border of hardy flowers, from Robinson's The English Flower Garden.

Munstead Wood, Surrey: Gertrude Jekyll's home and the first project on which she worked with Edwin Lutyens. This photograph was taken in 1984. The planting has changed since Jekyll's time and the clematis montana *which veiled the building has gone.*

The influence which Jekyll had on garden design came about not only through her writing, but also through her partnership with a third arts and crafts architect: Edwin Lutyens. They met in 1890 when he was only twenty-one and she was forty-seven. They soon formed a warm friendship which developed into a most productive working partnership. It was founded on a genuine 'closeness of minds' and shared a belief in 'the divinity of hard work'.[21] Jekyll had fully absorbed Repton, Price and Knight's theories of outdoor design and passed this knowledge on to the young Lutyens. When merged with their joint love for the vernacular arts and crafts it produced an approach to house and garden design which is described by Christopher Hussey:

> The whole approach of the young Lutyens to architecture, through his study of the landscape, traditions, and vernacular techniques of his home county [Surrey], was in the romantic tradition that regards buildings as properly the product of their soil and of the country craftsman's lore; and their planning as properly ordered by the circumstances of the site and the needs of their inhabitants.[22]

Jekyll and Lutyens enjoyed touring Surrey together in a pony cart and liked to discuss the materials, design and construction of the things they saw. Jekyll later

Part of William Robinson's wild garden at Gravetye Manor. His book, The Wild Garden, *1870, extolled the virtues of naturalistic planting. He remarked that he had 'never heard' of Uvedale Price, though his theory of wild planting was an unwitting return to Price's principles of planting design.*

Deanery Garden, Berkshire: a masterpiece by Jekyll and Lutyens. Photograph c.1912. The garden is being restored.

asked Lutyens to help design a new house in her garden at Munstead Wood. Construction began in 1895 and the project became a masterpiece. It is easy to think that Lutyens designed the house and Jekyll the garden, but this appears not to have been the case: it was a joint project. Lutyens had the technical knowledge but Jekyll had the strongest feeling concerning the character and proportions of the spaces which ought to be made. This applied equally to house and garden.

The close working relationship which produced Munstead Wood grew more distant as the years passed, but in the two decades before the First World War Lutyens and Jekyll created a number of houses and gardens which are among the most delightful to have been made in this country. They have a ripe old English charm which satisfies a deep-felt yearning for a civilised life in the country. When compared with the stately homes of earlier times they seem closer to Abraham Cowley's seventeenth century dream of rural retirement:

> I might be master at last of a small house and large garden, with moderate conveniences joined to them, and there dedicate the remainder of my life only to the culture of them and the study of nature.[23]

He would surely have found contentment at Munstead Wood, Orchards, Deanery Garden, Folly Farm or Hestercombe, all country retreats where the gardens provide a perfect setting for the houses, and the houses a perfect adornment to the gardens (pp. 184 and 185). Jane Brown describes them as 'the gardens of a golden afternoon',[24] and contrasts them with the later projects on which Jekyll was less involved and often did no more than a planting plan —

sometimes she did not even visit the site. Without Jekyll's guiding influence Lutyens' garden designs tended to become bleak and formal. Grandeur took the place of charm. At Gledstone Hall, 1922, and Tyringham, 1924, the gardens are ornaments to the buildings with little use or beauty of their own — Lutyens did not enjoy gardening, or even sitting about in gardens.

Castle Drogo, which was completed in 1929, is a particularly interesting Lutyens' project. One feels that the ghosts of Price, Knight and Repton might have had a hand in its conception. Price would have guided the client to choose the Picturesque site, and Knight the castellated architectural style. Judging from an early sketch, which is on display in the castle, Repton guided Lutyens' first scheme for the garden: it steps down a hillside like the garden which he designed for Bayham Abbey (p.116). However, Repton followed Vitruvius at Bayham and recomended the avoidance of hill-top sites because they are too exposed. Castle Drogo sits astride a hill top and the prevailing wind forced Lutyens to lay out an enclosed garden which lurks behind a great yew hedge in an attempt to find shelter.

The style which was brought to perfection by Jekyll and Lutyens achieved great popularity with amateur and professional gardeners. Its leading professional exponent, T.H. Mawson, was eight years older than Lutyens but started his career as a garden designer at almost the same time, c.1890. He lacked Lutyens' genius but was a very competent and prolific designer. Mawson took Repton and Kemp as his models and quoted Repton's principles for achieving 'formality near

The enclosed flower garden at Castle Drogo, Devon. The great yew hedge protects the garden from the winds which blow around the hill-top site.

Pampas grass, seen here in a 1960s' garden designed by Philip Hicks, was always greatly admired by William Robinson, who wrote that when well grown it is 'unsurpassed by anything that requires protection in frosty weather'.

The garden at Graythwaite Hall, in the Lake District, was designed by T.H. Mawson in 1896. It is a classic example of the style which Mawson expounded in The Art and Craft of Garden Making, *1900, and dedicated to the owner of Graythwaite. Mawson lacked Lutyens' genius but was a prolific designer and the leading professional exponent of the Arts and Crafts Style perfected by Jekyll and Lutyens. He believed in using local materials and traditional detailing.*

the house, merging into the natural by degrees, so as to attach the house by imperceptible gradations to the general landscape'[25] (p.126). In 1900 he had the idea of publishing a book on *The Art and Craft of Garden Making* which caught the mood of the day and provides us with a name for the style: Mawson interpreted the old English tradition of garden making in terms of the arts and crafts movement (p.182 and 183). The book was handsomely produced and, as Mawson proclaimed on the title page, it was 'Illustrated by photographic views and perspective drawings by C.E. Mallows and others, also chapter headings designed by Mr. D. Chamberlain, and one hundred and thirty plans and details of gardens designed by the author'.

The use of photographs in a book on garden design was an original idea which many publishers copied. A great series of picture books from *Country Life, The Studio* and other publishing houses followed.[26] They have left historians with a fine visual record of the state of English gardening at a time when vast resources were available for the construction and maintenance of country houses and gardens. This was the twilight hour of the wealthy landowning class which had so long patronised the art of landscape design. Like ageing fruit trees which

A HERTFORDSHIRE HOUSE AND GARDEN ❀ ❀ ❀ ❀ T·H·MAWSON

Mawson's design for a Hertfordshire garden in the Arts and Crafts Style, from his book The Art and Craft of Garden Making. *Note the vernacular detailing and the use of clipped hedges to form a series of compartments.*

Wood House, Devon, designed by T.H. Mawson.

Graythwaite Hall has an Arts and Crafts Style garden by T.H. Mawson. He was influenced by Repton and Kemp, and aimed for formality near the house 'merging into the natural by degrees'.

produce a fine harvest when they are destined not to survive another season, the country landowners of England produced one last crop of magnificent gardens before succumbing to income tax, estate duty and war.

In the early years of the Arts and Crafts Style, garden detailing was based on a patriotic admiration for the old English gardens which inspired the engravings of steps, walls, gateways and other features in Blomfield's book *The Formal Garden in England,* 1892. Further research showed the origin of many of these details to be Italian, and the style tended to drift into a third period of Italian influence over English gardens (pp.186-190).

Inigo Triggs' major study of *Formal Gardens in England and Scotland,* 1902, contains many examples of gardens which were made during the seventeenth and nineteenth century phases of Italian influence. They stimulated further historical research and new garden designs. Sir George Sitwell admired Blomfield's and Triggs' books and also knew that his family had owned an enclosed

The twilight of the country house garden captured by G.D. Leslie, R.A. (1835-1921), in his painting 'In Time of War'.

Above, Folly Farm, Berkshire, has been described as 'one of the most famous and most loved gardens of the partnership between Jekyll and Lutyens'. Courtesy Marian Thompson.

Right, the rill at Hestercombe, Somerset. Jekyll and Lutyens combined to create this delightful house and garden, now owned by the Somerset Fire Brigade. The garden is being restored to its original plan and planting.

The Italian garden at Hever Castle, Kent, was laid out in the 1920s for Lord Astor. The Arts and Crafts Style led to a third phase of Italian influence over English gardens lasting from c.1910-35.

Buscot Park, Berkshire, designed by Harold Peto in the Italian version of the Arts and Crafts Style. The rill forms the axis of the garden.

Hever Castle: a view of the Italian garden which contains a fine collection of antique sculpture.

Two views of The Hill, Hampstead, designed by T.H. Mawson for Lord Leverhulme in an Italian version of the Arts and Crafts Style. The elaborate Italian garden, though in need of restoration, reflects the grandeur which attracted clients to this style in the early decades of the twentieth century. The pergola, right, leads to a part of the garden which is now a public park, adjoining Hampstead Heath.

Sir George Sitwell's Italian garden at Renishaw, Derbyshire. It is still in good condition and owned by the Sitwell family.

garden in the seventeenth century. Sitwell spent many years studying Italian gardens, wrote a book on the subject,[27] and then spent a fortune laying out two gardens in an Arts and Crafts version of the Italian Style — at Renishaw in Derbyshire and at Montegufoni in Italy. Clients were attracted to the Italian Style by its air of grandeur and it was adopted by a large number of arts and crafts designers, including Inigo Thomas, H.A. Tipping, Oliver Hill and Harold Peto. Thomas Mawson laid out an elaborate Italian garden for Lord Leverhulme (pp.188 and 189). He also designed a 'cottage garden' for him in Lancashire at Roynton Cottage. It was built in the Arts and Crafts Style but using stone instead of brick in a most imaginative way.

Gardeners who undertook their own designs tended to remain loyal to the English version of the Arts and Crafts Style. The owner-designers of Great Dixter (N. Lloyd), Sissinghurst (V. Sackville-West), Hidcote (L. Johnston), and Kiftsgate (H. Muir) employed the style with great flair, and showed a sustained brilliance in their use of plant material which cannot be equalled by a designer who is not in residence. They followed in the wake of Gertrude Jekyll, who was also an owner-designer and, as Hussey justly observes,'the greatest *artist* in horticulture and garden-planting that England has produced'.[28]

Jekyll's theory of planting design can be traced to Knight, Price and Repton who published their first books in 1794/5. She combined Knight's admiration for native woods with Repton's idea of creating different compartments, and with Price's idea of basing the composition of planting schemes on landscape painting. Her interpretation of these three themes is expressed in the following quotations from her most successful book, *Colour Schemes for the Flower Garden*:

> On woods: I am myself surprised to see the number and wonderful variety of the pictures of sylvan beauty that [the wood] displays throughout the year. I did not specially aim at variety, but, guided by the natural conditions of each region, tried to think out how best they might be fostered and perhaps a little bettered.[29]

> On compartments: It is extremely interesting to work out gardens in which some special colouring predominates...it opens out a whole new range of garden delights...besides my small grey garden I badly want others, and especially a gold garden, a blue garden and a green garden.[30]

> On garden pictures: When the eye is trained to perceive pictorial effect, it is frequently struck by something — some combination of grouping, lighting and colour — that is seen to have that complete aspect of unity

A bridge at Roynton Cottage, Lancashire, built of local stone. This is in the 'cottage garden' designed by Mawson for Lord Leverhulme.

Three contemporary paintings of Gertrude Jekyll's garden at Munstead Wood, Surrey. Top, a watercolour by George S. Elgood, R.I. (1851-1943), of the white, pale blue and mauve Michaelmas daisy border. The two paintings by Katherine Montagu Wyatt (fl. 1889-1903), show, left, the sequence from pale blue and grey to golden yellow and blood red in the herbaceous border and, right, the Jekyll planting and Lutyens detailing of the grounds and house.

and beauty that to the artist's eye forms a picture. Such are the impressions that the artist-gardener endeavours to produce in every portion of the garden.[31]

J.M.W. Turner was the landscape painter Jekyll most admired. Her main border at Munstead Wood, and a great many of her other planting schemes, were designed to create a sequence from blood red in the centre, to golden yellow, to lemon yellow, to the white of the moon and to the pale blue of the sky. An identical sequence can be found in *The Fighting Temeraire* and many of Turner's later paintings. The influence of the French Impressionists on Jekyll's planting schemes has been very much exaggerated.[32]

The near-destruction of Jekyll's garden at Munstead Wood is a great loss to the nation's heritage, and is hardly compensated by the restorations in progress at Hestercombe, Great Maytham, New Place, and a number of other gardens.

Sissinghurst, Hidcote and Great Dixter are also in the Jekyll-Lutyens style. These gardens have attracted enormous numbers of visitors since 1946 and contributed to the continuing popularity of the style amongst amateur gardeners. The allegiance of such recent authors as G.E. Whitehead, K. Midgeley and Brigadier C.E. Lucas-Phillips, who have written for the amateur market, is revealed by their choice of illustrations — though they have interpreted the style with a marked lack of imagination. Garden styles are classified baldly as formal or informal. The Brigadier advises: 'If you aim at a very formal design, straight lines are the thing, but otherwise think in terms of soft, smooth-flowing curves...but no snaky wriggles, please'.[33] These authors have also been reluctant to use new materials. Whitehead observes: 'There have been many changes since I first started. Materials are different. Instead of natural stone we must use artificial pavings more often than not'.[34]

The continuing popularity of the Arts and Crafts Style in the 1980s can best be explained by its wide cultural base. The arts and crafts movement embodied an approach to life and work which is especially close to the historic gardening ideal of combining use with beauty, profit with pleasure and work with contemplation. This philosophy was adopted by William Morris and the community which he describes in *News from Nowhere*.[35] It was an ideal pastoral community which operated without laws or money. Morris enjoyed gardening and explains something of his approach to life and gardening in the following letter to Mrs. Burne-Jones:

> I am just going to finish my day with a couple of hours' work on my lecture [on the history of pattern-design] but will first write you a line...Yet it sometimes seems to me as if my lot was a strange one: you see, I work pretty hard, and on the whole very cheerfully, not altogether for pudding, still less for praise; and while I work I have the cause [of art] always in my mind...Well, one thing I long for which will certainly come, the sunshine and spring. Meantime we are hard at work gardening here: making dry paths, and a sublimely tidy box edging.[36]

The Arts and Crafts Style has also been able to satisfy the scientific interest in nature which has grown with such speed since Darwin's time. William Robinson was the first to advocate the conservation of wild flower meadows. In *The Wild*

A small Arts and Crafts Style garden in London — the changes in level, lush planting, rill and curved brick steps are characteristic features.

Garden he asks: 'Who would not rather see the waving grass with countless flowers than a close shaven surface without a blossom?'[37] As the possessor of a handsome Victorian beard he was able to add that shaving one's grass was as foolish as shaving one's face.

Robinson also encouraged an appreciation for the old gardens which were attached to that best-loved of British building types: the country cottage. He toured cottage gardens and illustrated them in his books and periodicals. In 1892 Robinson started a magazine on *Cottage Gardening* and announced that: 'To those who look at a garden from an artistic point of view the cottage garden is often far more beautiful than the gentleman's garden near it'.[38] (pp.196 and 213.) Brenda Colvin's garden at Filkins (p.213) is a lovely example of a modern cottage garden by an owner-designer. It has a Robinsonian flower meadow and is planted in the Arts and Crafts Style. Her partner, Hal Moggridge, describes the garden as follows:

It is a subtle blend of many different plants held together by a strong

Opposite, two views of Sissinghurst, Kent. This is the best known and most visited garden in the Arts and Crafts Style, and the continuing popularity of the style has helped to keep the original planting. However, those who knew the planting in Vita Sackville-West's time say that it has deteriorated. Both illustrations show the idea of compartments with rich planting.

A town garden beside Kew Green, in London, with traditional cottage garden planting.

overall composition; at every time of year the rich textures of foliage are lightened by many flowers always in perfect colour relationship to one another. To obtain this balance of form and colour individual plants have always been treated with determination.[39]

The treatment of plant forms, textures and colours as compositional elements foreshadows the Abstract Style.

The Abstract Style

The response of English garden design to modern art was exceptionally slow. In the first half of the twentieth century the overwhelming popularity of the Arts and Crafts Style formed a great wall which shielded garden designers from the explosion of creative energy that produced the Modern Movement in architecture and the fine arts. Since painting has been a vital influence on English garden design for two centuries, it is odd that so few designers peered over the wall to see what was happening to the other applied arts. In Europe and America the response of garden designers to modern art was faster. By 1900 Gaudie had shown at the Parc Güell in Barcelona[40] that art noveau, then known in Britain as the 'modern style', was peculiarly suited to the layout of parks and gardens, and by 1910 Frank Lloyd Wright's design for the Robie house in Chicago had shown that

196

the lines of a modern building could be extended to control the layout of outdoor space.

The landowning class which commissioned the great English gardens of the period showed no taste for stylistic innovation in their twilight hour. Nor is there any reason to think that garden designers had a significant interest in modern art before 1925. The Modern Movement was assailed by the leading designers of the day when it appeared over the skies of England. In 1916 Thomas Mawson was still laughing at the 'art nouveau craze' and lectured on 'the ridiculous ornament and the exaggerated design which this over-enthusiastic cult produced'.[41] In 1934 Sir Reginald Blomfield (he was knighted in 1919) wrote a book attacking the Modern Movement, in which he stated that 'our younger generation, trained exclusively in our architectural schools, are convinced that they are introducing a new era in architecture' and saw it as his loyal duty 'to do what I can to rescue a noble art from the degradation into which it seems to be sinking'.[42]

In 1953, when Peter Shepheard wrote a book on *Modern Gardens,* it was still necessary to look abroad for examples of private gardens which had been influenced by modern art.[43] Shepheard's foreign examples included gardens by Thomas Church and Burle Marx. The only convincingly modern English garden in the book, at Halland in Sussex, was designed by an architect and a landscape architect who had both emigrated to the United States. The architect, Serge Chermayeff, was Russian by birth and also owned the house. The landscape architect, Christopher Tunnard, was a pioneer of modern gardens in England. The illustrations in Shepheard's book demonstrate beyond question that it is possible to design gardens which can stand as totally modern works of art, but it would be difficult, even today, to fill a book with examples of wholly modern English gardens.

The main reason for describing the new style as 'abstract' is that it draws

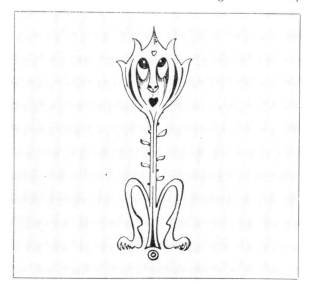 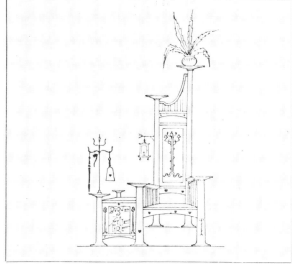

Two of T.H. Mawson's 'slides' which make fun of the art nouveau style.
Courtesy Royal Institute of British Architects.

Left, 'Composition with Red, Yellow and Blue' by Piet Mondrian. Compare this with the illustration on the right which shows the front cover of the first issue of De Stijl *magazine, 1917. The title and graphics resemble a modern garden plan.*
Mondrian Courtesy Haags Gemeentemuseum, The Hague.

inspiration from the abstract geometry of modern art. A subsidiary reason is that modern gardens have been divorced from the historical and literary references which were the starting point for all previous styles of English garden design. This corresponds to the early twentieth century painters' desire to produce a new art which was objective, analytical and non-figurative. Since there was a tendency to abstraction in primitive art it is tempting to name the new style of garden design after one of the four modern movements in art which have had most influence on garden designers. One could describe it as the cubist style, the constructivist style,

An abstract garden in Belgium by Jean Canneel-Claes, illustrated in Shepheard's *Modern Gardens.*

the neo-plastic style or the expressionist style. My reason for not using any of these names is that they would imply too close an identification with the somewhat wordy objectives of a particular group of artists.

Cubism is the parent of modern painting and also the movement which has had the most profound influence on garden design. Its starting point is generally taken to be the work of Cézanne and his intention of 'doing over Poussin entirely from nature'.[44] Cézanne went on to speak of art being 'theory developed and applied in contact with nature' and of treating nature 'by the cylinder, the sphere, the cone, everything in proper perspective so that each side of an object is directed towards a central point'. It is evident that there is a close affinity between this intention and the Neoplatonic theory of art which, as was discussed in the first chaper, produced the

Abstract paving pattern in black and white at Wexham Springs, Buckinghamshire.

A clay maquette for a landform design by Karen Moylan.

geometrically organised paintings and gardens of the seventeenth century.

Between 1910 and 1930 a group of Dutch artists, who described themselves as neo-plasticists, developed cubism into a totally non-figurative art. The leading figure in the movement was Piet Mondrian. He had painted realistic landscapes as a young man but came into contact with the cubist paintings of Braque and Picasso between 1911 and 1914. At the outbreak of war he returned to Holland and, in association with Theo van Doesburg, developed a rigorous non-figurative art. During his cubist period Mondrian had given his paintings titles which referred to figurative subjects, such as 'The Sea' and 'Horizontal Tree'. After formulating the principles of neo-plasticism he used titles which implied no subject, such as 'Composition', or 'Composition with Red, Yellow and Blue'. The theory which underpinned Mondrian's work was developed in conversation with M.H.J. Schoenmeakers,[45] a Dutch philosopher who created a link between the *De Stijl* movement and Plato's theory of forms (discussed in Chapter I). As in the seventeenth century it was believed that art should look upwards from the world of the particulars to the universal forms. Theo van Doesburg, the editor of *De Stijl,* explained the basis of the new art:

> As contrasted with traditional painting, where particularisation was of primary importance, painting in our time considers generalisation, that is to say the uncovering of the purely aesthetic in plastic features, as its principle value'.[46]

Van Doesburg believed that art should concentrate on the primary colours and forms, and 'leave the repetition of stories, tales, etc., to poets and writers'.[47]

The front cover which was used for the first issues of *De Stijl* resembles a modern garden plan. It was designed by Vilmos Huszar,[48] a founder member of the De Stijl group, and published in October 1917. The design could be made into a

200

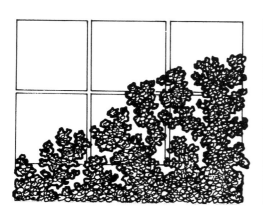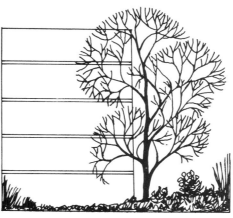

Patterns formed by geometrical and biological lines are a feature of modern gardens.

garden by translating the black and white pattern into paths, steps, raised beds, pools and stepping stones. Even the words 'De Stijl', which lie above the design, could be used to make a paving pattern with dark and light slabs. No such literal translation of a graphic design into a garden plan has been attempted, but the geometry of neo-plasticism has had a profound influence on the design of paved areas (p.216). When working with a T-square and set square it is easy to attempt Mondrian-type patterns.

The design of landform and the layout of planting areas has been more influenced by cubist sculpture. It is normal practice to execute such designs with a soft pencil or to make a maquette in clay.[49] Both media lend themselves to the kind of shapes and patterns which are seen in the work of Jean Arp, Constantin Brancuzi, Henry Moore, and Barbara Hepworth. They make considerable use of what might be described as muscular organic curves.

A biological planting pattern offset by a geometrical paving pattern. Designed by John Brookes, this example is influenced by cubist and neo-plastic art.

A curvilinear garden designed by J. St. Bodfan Gruffydd, 1960. The area beyond the paving can be compared to the curvilinear area in the drawing opposite.
Courtesy John Brookes.

A paved area in a Blackheath, London, garden. In modern gardens the transition from a rectilinear area to a curvilinear area is often achieved by the use of paving.

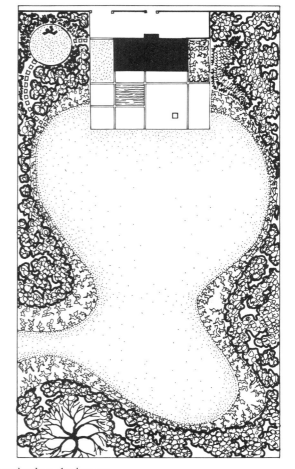

The Abstract Style: it is based on the shapes and patterns of abstract painting and sculpture.

Modern planting design has tended to be non-geometric and expressive. Designers have considered plants as abstract shapes and patches of colour, and have used them as a foil to the geometry of neo-plastic and cubist art. The inspiration for this device is uncertain, but the images which can be formed by overlaying random biological patterns on a structured geometrical background are highly characteristic of modern gardens (p.201). The two possible sources for the imagery are Japanese gardens and abstract expressionism. The former are known to have influenced particular designers, while the latter is a movement which has educated us all in the appreciation of abstract and random patterns.

The drawing of the Abstract Style shows a transition from a rectilinear paved area into a curvilinear planted area. It is intended for comparison with the previous drawings, but it must be remembered that it represents a garden of perhaps as little as 0.1 hectares, while some of the earlier drawings show estates of one thousand hectares and more. In many cases the modern paved area will be no more than a patio outside a French window, but even here the use of 600 x 600mm concrete slabs with prominent joints reminds one of the *De Stijl* aesthetic.

England was engaged on the Italian phase of the Arts and Crafts Style when the first modern gardens were being designed in Europe. In his autobiography, Russell Page looks back on the English gardens which were made between 1900 and 1930. He criticises them for employing 'a ragbag of styles [which have] nothing to do with real style'.[50] He and other designers were attracted to the classical gardens of France and Italy by their abstract spatial qualities. The beautiful pen and wash drawings in J.C. Shepherd and G.A. Jellicoe's *Italian Gardens of the Renaissance* reveal the spatial quality of the old gardens, and the authors remark that 'the bases of abstract design, running through history like a silver thread, are independent of race and age'.[51] Two years later, a second book, *Gardens and Design,* by the same authors, illustrated a house and garden by Frank Lloyd Wright and praised him for grasping 'the colossal latent power that lies behind the subject'.[52] A series of articles by Jellicoe appeared in *Architects' Journal* during 1931 and 1932.[53] The designs were classical but the discussion is highly analytical. In 1933 Jellicoe and Page were commissioned by Ronald Tree to

Ditchley Park, Oxfordshire, 1933, by G.A. Jellicoe, was the last major Italian garden to be designed in England. The large lawn was formerly occupied by an elaborate parterre.

The frontispiece to The Studio's 1932 Garden Annual *was J.C. Shepherd's own garden at Patching, Sussex.*

The restaurant in the Cheddar Gorge, by G.A. Jellicoe and R. Page, had one of the earliest modern gardens in England.
Courtesy Architectural Press Ltd.

design an Italian garden at Ditchley Park. The owner specifically wanted an Italian garden and Jellicoe comments:

> I had certainly studied the Italian garden in detail, but except for abortive designs for a new landscape at Claremont some years previously, my experience in the actual design and execution of the classics was nil. My aesthetic inclinations, indeed, were wholly for the modern movement in art, fostered by teaching at the Architectural Association's School of Architecture...Casting aside therefore all thoughts of twentieth-century art, of Picasso and Le Corbusier and Frank Lloyd Wright, I threw myself enthusiastically into a unique study of landscape history made real.[54]

Ditchley Park was the last major English garden to be designed in the Italian style. During the 1930s Jellicoe received a number of smaller commissions which provided an opportunity to introduce elements of the Abstract Style. The frontispiece to The Studio's 1932 *Garden Annual* shows a garden by Jellicoe's partner, J.C. Shepherd which has a distinctly modern flavour,[55] and in 1933 Jellicoe and Page worked together on the design of a restaurant and garden in the Cheddar Gorge.[56] The project was widely illustrated in the 1930s as an example of modern architecture.

Christopher Tunnard was the first English author to urge a connection between

A photograph by Tunnard of a Japanese garden whose lack of superfluous ornament has 'a special appeal to the modern mind of all countries'.

New Ways, a modern house by Peter Behrens standing in an older style garden with a Jekyllesque dry-stone wall — a strange combination.
Courtesy Architectural Press Ltd.

Bentley Wood at Halland, Sussex, where the garden was designed by Tunnard: a modern house in a modern garden.
Courtesy Architectural Press Ltd.

modern art and garden design. He published an article on Japanese gardens in *Landscape and Garden* in 1935 and said that their lack of superflous ornament has 'a special appeal to the modern mind of all countries'.[57] In 1938 he wrote a series of articles for the *Architectural Review* which attracted considerable attention and was republished as *Gardens in the Modern Landscape*. It became an important textbook which is often referred to by garden designers who trained in the 1950s as 'the only book we had'. Tunnard opens with the assertion 'A garden is a work of art'[58] and soon reveals himself as a true disciple of the Modern Movement. In 1937 he had even co-authored a manifesto on garden design with an international comrade. Tunnard and Jean Canneel-Claes proclaimed:

> We believe in the probity of the creative act . . . the reliance of the designer
> on his own knowledge and experience and not on the academic symbolism
> of the styles or outworn systems of aesthetics, to create by experiment and
> invention new forms which are significant of the age from which they
> spring.[59]

Tunnard believed that garden designers should 'return to functionalism' and he used quotations from le Corbusier: 'The styles are a lie',[60] and Adolf Loos: 'To find beauty in form instead of making it depend on ornament is the goal to which humanity is aspiring'.[61] Above all he believed that 'the modern house requires modern surroundings, and in most respects the garden of today does not fulfil this need'.[62] His point was well made by a photograph of a crisp white rectangular modern house in Northampton, by Peter Behrens, which looks most uncomfortable perched, as it is, on top of a Jekyllesque dry-stone wall and

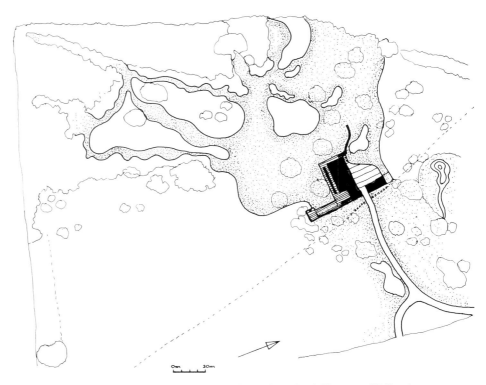

Christopher Tunnard's design for the garden of Bentley Wood House at Halland.

The Henry Moore sculpture at Halland influenced the pattern of the garden plan above.
Courtesy Architectural Press Ltd.

approached by a semi-circular flight of steps which 'fail entirely to harmonise with the character of the house'.[63] Many designers agreed with Tunnard but the public did not — the Behrens house was in fact the first in England to be designed in the international style. The public seem to have looked at Tunnard's photograph and decided that the garden was delightful but the house an abomination.

The kind of garden which ought to accompany a modern building was illustrated by a photograph of the house and garden at Halland designed by Chermayeff and Tunnard (p.207). It is an austerely beautiful and entirely modern design. The garden owes nothing to 'the second stone age with its plethora of flagged paths and dry walls'.[64] A sculpture in the garden by Henry Moore helped to make another of Tunnard's points:

> The best of contemporary architecture is closely related to the best of modern sculpture and constructivist painting because architects, sculptors and constructivist painters are in written or personal contact with one another.[65]

This was one of the fundamental principles on which the Bauhaus School had been founded. Walter Gropius stated in 1919:

> Let us create a new guild of craftsmen, without the class distinctions which raise an arrogant barrier between craftsmen and artist. Together, let us conceive and create the new building of the

A Jekyllesque planting scheme of the type which designers have often used as a foil to the abstract geometry of modern art (pp.202 and 203).

future, which will embrace architecture *and* sculpture *and* painting in one unity and which will one day rise toward heaven from the hands of a million workers, like the crystal symbol of a new faith.[66]

The Halland project became the crystal symbol of a new faith for English garden designers.

The most important British design school to adopt the new faith was the Architectural Association (A.A.) in London. Tunnard was a member of the Modern Architecture Research Group (M.A.R.S.) which was based at the A.A. and played an important part in introducing modern architecture to England (p.217). Tunnard was probably also the author of a 1938 arcticle in *Landscape and Garden*, by 'A member of the Mars Group', which proclaimed that if 'lofty buidings, flat roofs, reinforced concrete and a remapping of the countryside' are 'necessary for the betterment of social conditions' then members of the Mars Group 'will not hesitate to advocate them'.[67] For a short time in the 1930s

Peter Shepheard's 'sitting room garden' at the Festival of Britain on London's South Bank, 1951, with York stone paths, loose cobbles, a grass lawn and herbaceous border.

members of the Group had made it possible to say 'that England leads the world in modern architectural activity'.[68] Staff and students at the A.A. were inspired to create modern buildings with modern surroundings. Geoffrey Jellicoe, Peter Shepheard and Hugh Casson were all connected with the A.A. in the 1930s and later became prominent members of the Institute of Landscape Architects (I.L.A.). Jellicoe was Principal of the A.A. from 1939 to 1942 and President of the I.L.A. from 1939 to 1949.

The future of the Abstract Style after World War II lay with the professional designers who joined the I.L.A. after its formation in 1929. Tunnard left England in 1939 to become a Professor of City Planning at Yale University, but his book was republished in 1948 and had a considerable influence on post-war designers in England and America.[69] The first major opportunity for English designers came with the Festival of Britain in 1951. Hugh Casson was design director and a number of landscape architects were employed on its gardens. They included Peter Shepheard, Russell Page, Peter Youngman and Frank Clark. Clark had worked with Tunnard on *Gardens in the Modern Landscape*[70] and was the leader of the only full-time landscape design course in the U.K. Youngman ran a part-time course at University College in London. A number of photographs of the Festival were included in Peter Shepheard's *Modern Gardens*. The hard detailing was clearly

The water gardens in Harlow New Town, designed by Sir Frederick Gibberd.

210

influenced by the *De Stijl* aesthetic, but the way in which it was enlivened by planting and water-washed stones appears to derive from Tunnard's analysis of Japanese gardens. Crisp geometry was offset by natural shapes and patterns.

Many of the designers who joined the I.L.A. before 1939 did so because of their interest in private gardens. After 1946 they found that few clients wished to commission garden designs. There was, however, a greatly increased demand for landscape designers to work in the public sector: on housing estates, new towns, reservoirs, factories and power stations (p.216). It was on these projects that the Abstract Style flourished in the 1950s and 1960s. They lie outside the scope of this book but are referred to by Tony Aldous and Brian Clouston in *Landscape by Design*.[71] There are many public spaces in the new towns which illustrate the style: in Harlow by F. Gibberd and S. Crowe, in Hemel Hempstead by G.A. Jellicoe, in Stevenage by G. Patterson, and in Cumbernauld by P. Youngman and W. Gillespie.

A number of books which illustrate the Abstract Style in private gardens have been aimed at the general public. In 1953 Lady Allen of Hurtwood and Susan Jellicoe wrote a book on *Gardens*[72] for Penguin Books. Lady Allen had worked with the New Homes For Old Group which supported the cause of modern architecture in the 1930s. The book contained photographs of gardens designed by Thomas Church, Garrett Eckbo, C. Th. Sorensen and other foreign pioneers of the Abstract Style.

In 1958 Sylvia Crowe published a book on *Garden Design*[73] which contains a masterly analysis of the abstract qualities of gardens in the chapters on the principles and materials of design. Her discussion of the Four Faces Urn at Bramham illustrates the analytical nature of her approach and her belief that 'underlying all the greatest gardens are certain principles of composition which remain unchanged because they are rooted in the natural laws of the universe'.[74] She continues:

> The long vista at Bramham Park, Yorkshire, looks across a pool and the end is marked by a huge urn. The two do not compete, but are complementary, forming together one composition. The dominant vertical figure is completed by the calm horizontal pool which does nothing to prevent the eye travelling easily on its way to the terminal point.[75]

This analysis contrasts with the eighteenth century associationist approach of Archibald Alison, who valued the urn at Hagley because it was 'chosen by Mr. Pope for the spot and now inscribed to his memory',[76] and also with the nineteenth century stylistic approach of Loudon and Kemp. Loudon advised that urns and statues should only be placed where they can be 'viewed in connection with some architectural production',[77] and Kemp that 'statuary, vases, and

The Four Faces Urn at Bramham, West Yorkshire, is taken by Sylvia Crowe to illustrate the abstract qualities of gardens which 'are rooted in the natural laws of the universe'.

Great Dixter, East Sussex, is a famous garden in the Arts and Crafts Style. A dry-stone wall and grass path mark the point of transition from the compartment gardens near the house to a Robinsonian wildflower meadow. The garden was planted by Christopher Lloyd, and influenced by Gertrude Jekyll.

Opposite top, Brenda Colvin's garden at Filkins, Oxfordshire, with flower-filled lawn. Opposite, a country cottage garden. Both were 'inspired by the Arts and Crafts Style and give their owners 'use with beauty, profit with pleasure and work with contemplation'.

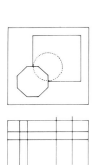

A modern garden by Sylvia Crowe at Wexham Springs, Buckinghamshire.
Courtesy Cement and Concrete Association.

Left, abstract garden patterns from John Brookes' Garden Design and Layout, *1970.*
Courtesy John Brookes.

Below, a courtyard by John Brookes, using traditional materials.

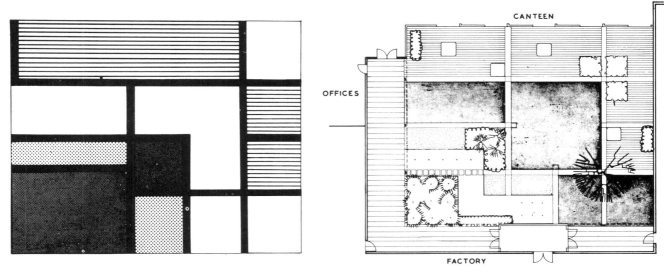

similar architectural ornaments, are the fitting associates of Grecian and Italian houses, and appear less suitable in relation to every other style'.[78] Examples of abstract designs by Sylvia Crowe can be seen at Wexham Springs in Buckinghamshire and the Commonwealth Institute in London.

John Brookes, who worked for a time in the office of Sylvia Crowe and Brenda Colvin, is the best known English designer to have applied abstract principles to gardens. His books have achieved an unusually wide readership and proved that gardens can be modern without resorting to the austerity of the house at Halland.[79] The photographs in his books show warm, friendly, useful spaces, while his plans and diagrams reveal the abstract geometrical patterns which have led to their spatial organisation. Brookes is a successful garden designer. His design for the Penguin Books' courtyard near Heathrow Airport is used in *Room Outside* to illustrate the point that 'looking at modern paintings can also help one to see how areas of colour and texture can be counter-positioned to form a balanced whole'.[80] The design was generated by a Mondrian-type drawing which was geared to the modular pattern of the building and then translated into areas of paving, grass, water and planting.

The Penguin Books' courtyard. The design was generated by a Mondrian-type drawing which was geared to the modular pattern of the building and then translated into paving, grass, water and planting.

215

Relations between the world of ideas and garden design remain important, though the inspiration now comes more from the fine arts and science than from literary or philosophical sources. Opposite, a Henry Moore sculpture in a parkland setting. Moore's work has had a considerable influence on planting and landform design. Opposite below, High Point, Highgate — a lofty modern building with a flat roof designed by Tecton, whose members also belonged to the M.A.R.S. Group. The constructivist aesthetic of the building is relieved by the caryatids and the generous planting.

Above, a patio garden by Michael Lancaster draws on the abstract geometry of modern art. Courtesy Michael Lancaster.

Below, the roof garden for Harvey's Store in Guildford, Surrey, was designed by G.A. Jellicoe. It is a beautiful abstract composition which was 'designed at the time when the first Sputnik spun miraculously round and far above the earth, and it was probably the implication of this that caused the whirl of circles...reminiscent of the planets'. Courtesy Susan Jellicoe.

In 1960 G.A. Jellicoe published the first of his three *Studies in Landscape Design*.[81] They are inspiring books and give examples of the way in which his own design projects have been influenced by modern artists, including Paul Klee, Jean Arp, Henry Moore, Ben Nicholson and Barbara Hepworth. The *Studies* were concerned with public sector projects, but in 1968 Susan and Geoffrey Jellicoe published a book which examines modern gardens from a similar standpoint. Jellicoe comments: 'Just as the mind is responding, in abstract art, to shapes which it appears to seek and even to crave, so it responds to shapes in landscapes'.[82] (See p. 217.) A major opportunity to apply this idea came with an invitation to prepare designs for the most significant private garden to have been made in England since the war. Jellicoe describes his meeting with the client as follows:

> My first visit was on 22 July, 1980. I remember nearly stumbling over a Henry Moore sculpture on the floor and observing a Ben Nicholson over the mantelpiece, with a huge Monet close by and a Graham Sutherland in the offing. I realised within a few minutes that Stanley Seeger and I were on the same wave-length in thinking that landscape art should be a continuum of past, present and future, and should contain within it the seeds of abstract ideas as well as having figurative meaning.[83]

This conjunction of a designer and a client sharing a passion for modern art has produced the *magnum opus* of modern English garden design: Sutton Place in Surrey. It contains a paradise garden based on a serpentine grid with fountains at the nodes, a secret moss garden with two hidden circles, a Magritte walk, a Miro swimming pool, a lake designed as the setting for a Henry Moore sculpture and a marble wall by Ben Nicholson. The latter (p.220) is a work of great beauty and respresents an artistic ideal which has had an overwhelming influence on the Abstract Style of garden design. Nicholson's work shows an affinity with Dutch neo-plasticism and emphasises the circle and square as the primary geometrical forms.

The last word on the Abstract Style should come from Tunnard, though he speaks of 'structure' and a 'grand conception' instead of 'style' — because of his functionalist belief that the, styles had been rendered obsolete. It can be set alongside the descriptions of the landscape ideal, which were quoted in the first chapter (pp.32-34), and is expressed with admirable directness:

> The author's personal approach to landscape gardening and planning has not changed. First, an eighteenth century understanding of 'the genius of the place' is necessary. Then the structure — in which usefulness and aesthetic pleasure must both be considered. Then materials of only the best quality (when they are available!) — this is very important, and it will be noticed that they are put in their proper place, after the grand conception, not before it. Finally, understanding the wishes of the client, whether it is a private citizen or a public committee in New York or London.[84]

Since a dislike of raw concrete is one of the main reasons for the unpopularity of modern construction, it is instructive to note Tunnard's insistence on the use of 'only the best' materials.

A cubist fence designed by Preben Jakobsen.
Courtesy Preben Jakobsen.

The marble wall by Ben Nicholson at Sutton Place, Surrey, is the most splendid example of abstract art in an English garden. It is a work of great beauty and represents an artistic ideal which has had an overwhelming influence on the abstract style of garden design.   Courtesy Marian Thompson.

Recent Trends

The Arts and Crafts and the Abstract Styles continue to dominate English garden design but they have begun to merge. The geometry of abstract art has been blended with the varied sensuous delights of arts and crafts gardens. This tendency is most apparent in the selection of materials. The coldness of square concrete slabs, white-painted wood, and steel, which once characterised the Abstract Style, have given way to the warmth of earthy bricks, stained timber and concrete finishes in which the cement is dominated by an exposed stone aggregate. Decorative fittings have reappeared in gardens and the prevailing sense of place and scale is altogether more intimate than in the early days of the Abstract Style.

Preben Jakobsen is a designer who has perfected the new approach. He writes as follows:

> I like to think that all my work is abstract art to a greater or lesser extent, in any project there are always some items which lend themselves to abstract treatment, such as paving, gates, etc. Lutyens and Aalto are great heroes of mine; what a combination you might think; of course I don't

like everything they did. C. Th. Sorensen always instilled in us that we should not copy other artists' work.[85]

Lutyens and Aalto make a fascinating combination. Both had an intuitive sense of geometry and a great interest in materials. The difference is that Lutyens looked backwards to tradition while Aalto looked forwards to the shapes and patterns of modern art. Jakobsen's own work (below and pp.219 and 222) shows a love of geometry and a fine discrimination in the choice of hard materials. He also exploits the colours, patterns and textures of plant material with imagination.

Planting design has often been the first element of gardens to be affected by the wind of change. It appears to be so once again. A new wave of naturalism, known to designers as the ecological, or conservation, approach, is influencing garden designers. The word 'ecological' is misleading, since ecology is an investigative science and not a design method, but it does convey the idea that planting schemes should have less artificiality and function according to the principles of a natural ecosystem. In other words there should be less weeding, less use of chemicals, and

A London garden by Preben Jakobsen who combines the abstract geometry of modern art with a taste for warm colours and rich-textured materials.

at the same time more native plants, more layers of plant growth, more species'
diversity and more exuberance. The resultant planting has the lushness of a
natural habitat, not the controlled regimentation of a traditional garden. From a
design point of view this approach can be seen as the recurrence of a desire for
'wild nature' which was present in the Forest and Irregular Styles, and the
Robinsonian wild garden.

It is an intriguing fact that part of the inspiration for this approach should have
come from England's old Protestant ally, Holland. A book by Alan Ruff, *Holland
and the Ecological Landscape,*[86] examines the Dutch approach. He traces its origins
to the *De Stijl* idea that design should be as functional and as free of ornament as
possible. This led to the use of exclusively native plants in the Amsterdam Bos

An abstract paving pattern with cobbles and lush planting by Preben Jakobsen.

A garden by Chris Baines, author of How to Make a Wildlife Garden, *1985. The visual diversity and nature conservation value of wildlife gardens have wide popular appeal.*
Courtesy Chris Baines.

Park in the 1930s, and to the creation of Heem parks after 1950. In the J.P. Thijsse Park, a Heem park named after one of the first advocates of native species, some very beautiful effects have been created with wild plants (p.224). They are achieved by an extraordinary reversal of traditional gardening practices: the topsoil is removed, no fertilisers or machines are used, plants are grown from native seeds and zones of very wet and very dry soil are encouraged. These methods require a greater expenditure of labour but a lower expenditure of capital. The conservation garden marks a step backwards from the technological garden and a return to the old idea that a garden should be a place to work and to contemplate the nature of the world. Two books, published in 1985, give practical advice on encouraging wild plants and animals in gardens.[87,88]

The most interesting pointer to the future of English garden design is the new awareness of gardening as a fine art. Two journals devoted to the history of gardening have been established and a considerable number of books on garden history have been published — one of them bearing the title *The Garden as a Fine Art.*[89] Three exhibitions with the title *Art into Landscape* were sponsored by the Arts Council in the 1970s and revealed a high level of public interest in the subject.[90] A most surprising feature of these exhibitions was the number of

Wild plants in the J.P. Thijsse Park, one of the Dutch Heem parks which have influenced the English ecological or conservation approach to garden design. The conservation garden harks back not only to the Forest and Irregular Styles, but also to the Robinsonian wild garden. It relies on the use of native plants and on a reversal of 'modern' gardening practice, by avoiding fertilisers, herbicides and intensive cultivation.

The concrete toadstools designed by Elizabeth Creasy. Courtesy Cement and Concrete Association.

entries from the general public which appear to have been inspired by pop art. A giant wash basin and a Brobdingnagian knot garden were proposed for a Thames-side site in Rotherhithe. Since many of the exhibits were visually successful it is puzzling that so little pop art should have found its way into gardens. One small but cheerful item to have done so is the red and white spotted toadstool designed by Elizabeth Creasy and her father. The booklet which explains how to make the toadstool was first published in 1979 and reprinted twice in 1982.[91]

There has also been a series of exhibitions which have stressed the essential link between the fine arts and gardening. The first, mounted by the Victoria and Albert Museum in 1979, was described as 'a celebration of one thousand years of British gardening'. In his introduction to the exhibition guide Hugh Johnson asks why it should be that 'this nation of gardeners has only just begun to review its own gardening past?',[92] and he goes on to observe that 'fashion has been as fickle in gardening as in architecture — if anything more so'. The second exhibition, devoted to Richard Payne Knight, reminded visitors of Knight's multifarious artistic interests — in gardening, architecture, painting, coin collecting and Greek sculpture. The third and fourth exhibitions, held in 1981, were concerned with the work of Gertrude Jekyll and Edwin Lutyens. They gave a further boost to the popularity of the Arts and Crafts Style. The fifth exhibition, of Humphry Repton's work, was devoted to a man who was equally talented as a painter, an author and a garden designer. His income came from all three arts. The sixth exhibition, held in 1983, dealt only with Lancelot Brown's work in the north of England. The catalogue restates the current estimation of 'Britain's most famous landscape gardener' as an English 'genius' who stands shoulder to shoulder with Edmund Burke and William Hogarth.[93] There have also been two exhibitions, in 1984 and 1985, of modern garden sculpture at High Wall, Oxford.

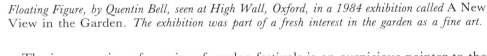

Floating Figure, by Quentin Bell, seen at High Wall, Oxford, in a 1984 exhibition called A New View in the Garden. *The exhibition was part of a fresh interest in the garden as a fine art.*

The inauguration of a series of garden festivals is an auspicious pointer to the future of English garden design. The festivals at Liverpool in 1984 and Stoke on Trent in 1986 will be followed by festivals at Glasgow in 1988, Gateshead in 1990 and a Welsh site in 1992. Such festivals are planned on a model which has proved highly successful in Europe. The Liverpool master plan owed more to the Mixed Style than to any of the other styles discussed in this book.[94] Lyall commented that 'anybody looking for anything remotely resembling a fresh international landscape theory and practice' would be disappointed by the master plan.[95] Half the site is to be retained as a public park and the other half, north of the spine road, will be used for residential and industrial purposes.

The importance of the Liverpool International Garden Festival in the history of English garden design rests upon its 'theme gardens'. The use of themes marks a complete departure from the non-representational Abstract Style, and implies a return to what van Doesburg described as 'the repetition of stories, tales, etc.', which he believed should be left to 'poets and writers'.[96] If new links are forged between garden design, contemporary art, philosophy and poetry, the consequences of the Festival will be salutary. If, on the other hand, the theme gardens merely lead to cheap reconstructions of historical styles, it will be a retrograde step. The art of garden design prospers when it looks to the fine arts and the world of ideas. It falters when looking exclusively to its own history.

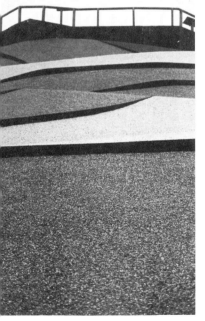

The gravel sculpture at the Liverpool International Garden Festival of 1984 is a self-assured exercise in abstract design.

The Liverpool International Garden Festival signified a departure from the Abstract Style of garden design: the master plan derived from the Mixed Style, and many of the individual gardens were designed round figurative 'themes'. Above, the Chinese Garden contained replicas of two Imperial buildings from Peking's Behai Park. Below, left and right, the British Garden was designed to 'illustrate the national character and build upon the British garden tradition' (Festival Guide p.115). National themes are well suited to a garden festival, but new and different themes will be appropriate in private gardens.

References and Notes

Chapter I (pp.9-43)

1. Genesis 2: 8, 9, 15.
2. Ibid., 3: 17-19.
3. Columella, L.J.M., *De Re Rustica,* H. Boyd Ash (trans.), Harvard, 1941, preface.
4. Røstvig, M.-S., *The Happy Man: Studies in the Metamorphosis of a Classical Idea,* 2nd edn., Oslo, 1962, p.42-3.
5. Virgil, *Eclogues and Georgics,* London, 1965, Everyman's Library, vol.222, bk.2, lines 589-621.
6. Masson, G., *Italian Gardens,* London, 1966, p.12.
7. Horace, 'Second Epode', A. Cowley (trans.), in A.R. Waller (ed.), *The English Writings of Abraham Cowley,* Cambridge, 1906, p.243.
8. Milton, J., *Paradise Lost,* bk.IV, lines 246-55.
9. Temple, W., *Works,* 'Upon the Gardens of Epicurus', 1814, vol.III, p.243.
10. Ibid., p.214.
11. Cooper, A.A., third Earl of Shaftesbury, *Characteristics of Men, Manners, Opinions, Times,* 'The Moralists', London, 1711, pt.2, section 4.
12. Cooper, A.A., third Earl of Shaftesbury, 'The Beautiful', in B. Rand, *The Life, Unpublished Letters, and Philosophical Regimen of Anthony, Earl of Shaftesbury,* London and New York, 1900, p.247.
13. Switzer, S., *Ichnographia Rustica,* London, 1718, vol.1, p.25.
14. Ibid., p.xv.
15. Pevsner, N., *Studies in Art, Architecture and Design,* London, 1969, vol.1, p.82. The abbreviated version of Temple's quotation comes from N. Pevsner, *The Englishness of English Art,* 1968, p.165. The passage is quoted in full as the last paragraph of the excerpt from Temple's essay in J.D. Hunt, and P. Willis (eds.), *The Genius of the Place,* London, 1975.
16. Burke, J., *English Art 1714-1800,* Oxford, 1976, p.40.
17. Hunt, J.D., and Willis, P. (eds.), *The Genius of the Place,* London, 1975, p.9.
18. D'Argenville, A.J. Dézallier, *La Théorie et la Pratique du Jardinage,* Paris, 1709 (anonymously), trans. by John James as *The Theory and Practice of Gardening,* 1712.
19. Switzer, S., op.cit., vol.1, p.40.
20. Ibid., preface, p.vii-viii.
21. Cooper, A.A., 'The Beautiful', p.246.
22. Cooper, A.A., *Characteristics...,* pt.3 section 2.
23. Leatherbarrow, D., 'Character, Geometry and Perspective: the Third Earl of Shaftesbury's Principles of Garden Design', *Journal of Garden History,* vol.4, no.4, pp.332-58.
24. Cooper, A.A., *Characteristics...,* pt.3, section 2.
25. Switzer, S., op.cit., vol.3, appendix.
26. Wooton, H., *The Elements of Architecture,* London, 1642.
27. Bacon, F., *The Essays, Colours of Good and Evil and Advancement of Learning of Francis Bacon,* 'Of Gardens', 1900 edn., London, p.113-18.
28. Lang, S., 'The Genesis of the English Landscape Garden', in N. Pevsner (ed.), *The Picturesque Garden and its Influence Outside the British Isles,* Washington, D.C., 1974, p.26.
29. Temple, W., op.cit., vol.III, p.235.
30. Cooper, A.A., *Characteristics...,* pt.3, section 2.
31. Switzer, S., op.cit., vol.2, p.201.
32. Lovejoy, A.O., *The Great Chain of Being,* Harper edn., New York, 1965, p.24.
33. Panofsky, E., *Gothic Architecture and Scholasticism,* London, 1957, p.44-5.
34. Wallis, R.T., *Neoplatonism,* London, 1972, p.163.
35. Wittkower, R., *Architectural Principles in the Age of Humanism,* London, 1962, p.22-32.
36. Pope, A., *An Epistle to Lord Burlington,* 1731.
37. Pope, A., 'On Gardens', *The Guardian,* Sept. 1713, no.173.
38. Pope, A., *An Essay on Criticism,* 1711.
39. Pope, A., 'On Gardens'.
40. Locke, J., *The Growth and Culture of Vines and Olives,* London, 1766.
41. Cooper, A.A., *Characteristics...,* pt.3, section 2.
42. Ibid.
43. Ibid.
44. Steuart, H., *Planter's Guide,* Edinburgh, 1828, p.422.
45. Gilpin, W.S., *Practical Hints upon Landscape Gardening,* London, 1832, p.102-5.
46. Steuart, H., op. cit., p.422.
47. Gilpin, W.S., op.cit., p.98.
48. Ibid., p.108.
49. Cooper, A.A., *Characteristics...,* pt.4, section 3.
50. DuFresnoy, C.A., *The Art of Painting,* London, 1695.
51. Clark, K., *Landscape into Art,* Penguin edn., London, 1956, p.67.
52. Ibid., p.83.
53. Nourse, T., *Campania Felix,* London, 1700. C. Thacker in *The History of Gardens,* London, 1979, p.103, has pointed out that Nourse's frontispiece resembles Falda's view of the Villa Pia.
54. Clifford, D., *A History of Garden Design,* London, 1962, p.123.
55. Dobrée, B., *English Literature in the Early Eighteenth Century 1700-1740,* Oxford, 1959, p.102-5.
56. Addison, J., *The Spectator,* essays 411-21, 1712.
57. Hussey, C., *English Gardens and Landscapes 1700-1750,* London, 1967, p.11.
58. Stroud, D., *Capability Brown,* 1957 edn., London, appendix III.
59. Price, U., *An Essay on the Picturesque, as compared with the Sublime and the Beautiful; and on the use of studying pictures, for the purpose of improving real landscape,* London, 1794, p.109.
60. Repton, H., *Fragments on the Theory and Practice of Landscape Gardening,* London, 1816, preface.
61. Jekyll, G., 'Gardens and Garden Craft', *Edinburgh Review,* July 1896, vol. 184, p.180.
62. Turner, T.H.D., 'Scottish Origins of Landscape Architecture', *Landscape Architecture,* May 1982, vol.72, no.3, p.52-5.
63. Geddes, P., *Cities in Evolution,* London, 1915, p.97.
64. Ibid., p.95-6.
65. McHarg, I.L., *Design with Nature,* 1971 edn., New York, p.5.
66. Ibid., p.151.
67. *A Supplement to the Oxford English Dictionary,* Oxford, 1976.
68. Hoskins, W.G., *The Making of the English Landscape,* London, 1955.
69. Salmon, W., *Polygraphice,* London, 1672, p.138.

70. Ibid., p.30.
71. Drayton, M., *Poly-olbion,* London, 1613, p.284.
72. Addison, J., *The Spectator,* essay 414, 1712.
73. Walpole, H., *The History of the Modern Taste in Gardening,* London, 1780.
74. Hunt, J.D., and Willis, P., op.cit., p.300.
75. Hume, D., *Enquiries concerning the human understanding and concerning the principles of morals,* L.A. Selby-Bigge (ed.), 2nd edn., Oxford, 1902, p.179.
76. Loudon, J.C. *Encyclopaedia of Gardening,* London, 1822, p.72.
77. Walpole, H., 'The History of the Modern Taste in Gardening', London, 1780.
78. Hunt, J.D., and Willis, P., op.cit., p.320.
79. Hussey, C., *The Picturesque,* 2nd edn., London, 1967, p.111.
80. Gilpin, W., *Three Essays on Picturesque Beauty, on Picturesque Travel and on Sketching Landscape,* London, 1792.
81. Knight, R.P., *The Landscape,* 2nd edn., London, 1795, pp.21-5.
82. Price, U., op.cit., p.246.
83. Ibid., p.251.
84. Loudon, J.C. (ed.), *The Landscape Gardening and Landscape Architecture of the Late H. Repton Esq.,* London, 1840, p.510.
85. Loudon, J.C., *Observations . . . on the Theory and Practice of Landscape Gardening, etc.,* Edinburgh, 1804, p.210. In view of the fact that Chambers had praised the wildness of Chinese gardens in 1757 it is odd that Loudon should include 'Chinese-like' as a criticism of Brown.
86. *The Quarterly Review,* March 1828, vol. xxxvii, p.315. The article is anonymous but was, in fact, written by Sir Walter Scott.
87. Mawson, T.H., *The Art and Craft of Garden Making,* 2nd edn., London, 1901, p.2.
88. Jekyll, G., *A Gardener's Testament,* London, 1937, p.30.
89. Holme, C. (ed.), 'The Gardens of England in the Southern and Western Counties', *The Studio,* 1907, p.xviii.
90. M.-L. Gothein's exhaustive history of garden art was first published in German in 1913. The second German edition was published in 1925 and the first English edition, from which this quotation is taken, was published in 1928 as *A History of Garden Art,* London, p.286.
91. Hussey, C., *The Picturesque,* p.137.
92. Ibid., p.58.
93. Stroud, D., *Capability Brown,* 1950 edn., London, p.13.
94. Pevsner, N., *An Outline of European Architecture,* 3rd edn., London, 1945, p.193.
95. Hoskins, W.G., *The Making of the English Landscape,* London, 1955, p.135.
96. Fairbrother, N., *New Lives, New Landscapes,* London, 1970, p.367.
97. The harshest critic of recent years has been Roy Strong who inscribed his book on *The Renaissance Garden in England,* London, 1979, as follows: 'In memory of all those gardens destroyed by Capability Brown and his successors'.
98. Hunt, J.D. and Willis, P., op.cit., p.105.
99. Geddes, P., *City Development,* Edinburgh, 1904, p.97.

Chapter II (pp.44-73)

1. Strabbo, W., 'Hortulus', trans. by R.S. Lambert as *Hortulus or The Little Garden,* London, 1923, p.37.
2. Strong, R., *The Renaissance Garden in England,* London, 1979.
3. Ibid., p.136.
4. Ibid., p.223.
5. Temple, W., *Works,* 'Upon the Gardens of Epicurus', 1814, vol. III, p.236.
6. Strong, R., op.cit., p.200.
7. Mollet, A., *Jardin de Plaisir,* 1651.
8. Evelyn, J., *Sylva, or a Discourse on Forest-Trees,* London, 1664.
9. Amherst, A., *London Parks and Gardens,* London, 1907, p.67.
10. Ibid., p.115.
11. Switzer, S., *Ichnographia Rustica,* London, 1718, gives a history of the firm in vol.1.
12. London, G., and Wise, H., *The Retir'd Gard'ner,* London, 1706.
13. Switzer, S., op.cit., vol.1, p.79.
14. Green, H., *Gardener to Queen Anne: Henry Wise (1635-1738) and the Formal Garden,* London, 1956, p.169.
15. John Harris suggests that the drawing might have been by Kip, and Christopher Hussey that it might have been by Knyff. See J. Harris, *The Artist and the Country House,* London, 1979, p.93, and C. Hussey, *English Gardens and Landscapes 1700-1750,* London, 1967, p.20.
16. Temple, W., op.cit.
17. Temple, W., op.cit., vol.I, p.xxvii.
18. Hussey, C., *English Gardens and Landscapes 1700-1750,* London, 1967, p.21.
19. Bacon, F., 'Of Gardens', 1625.
20. Strong, R., op.cit., p.42.
21. Parkinson, J., *Paridisi in Sole Paradisus Terrestris,* 1629.
22. Gerard, J., *Herball,* 1597.
23. Kip, J., and Knyff, L., *Britannia Illustra or Views of Several of the Queen's Palaces, also of the Principal Seats of the Nobility and Gentry of Great Britain,* 1707.

Chapter III (pp.74-112)

1. Switzer, S., *Ichnographia Rustica,* London, 1718, vol.1, p.xv. The italics in the quotation are the author's.
2. Ibid., 1742 edn., vol.1, p.41.
3. Ibid., 1742 edn., vol.1, p.xvi.
4. Switzer, S., *The Practical Kitchen Gardener,* London, 1727, Dedication.
5. Pope, A., *Ode on Solitude,* 1717.
6. Hussey, C., *English Gardens and Landscapes 1700-1750,* London, 1967, p.80.
7. Willis, P., *Charles Bridgeman and the English Landscape Garden,* London, 1977, p.1.
8. Hussey, C., op.cit., p.123.
9. Switzer, S., *Ichnographia Rustica,* p.124.
10. Ibid., p.40.
11. Hussey, op.cit., p.61.
12. Thorne, J.O. (ed.), *Chambers Biographical Dictionary,* 1969 edn., Edinburgh, p.66.
13. Pope, A., 'On Gardens', *The Guardian,* Sept. 1713, no.173.

14. Pope, A., *An Epistle to Lord Burlington,* 1731.
15. Walpole, H., *The History of the Modern Taste in Gardening,* London, 1780.
16. Ibid.
17. Ibid.
18. Hussey, C., op.cit., p.116.
19. Hunt, J.D., and Willis, P. (eds.), *The Genius of the Place,* London, 1975, p.232.
20. Woodbridge, K., *The Stourhead Landscape,* The National Trust, 1971, p.11.
21. *The World,* 13 Dec., 1753, no.50.
22. Hogarth, W., *The Analysis of Beauty,* London, 1753.
23. Dodsley, J., *Letters written by the Right Honourable Lady Luxborough to William Shenstone Esq.,* London, 1775, p.379.
24. Stroud, D., *Capability Brown,* 1975 edn., London, p.214.
25. Christopher Thacker attributes the design of the Doric temple to Brown (*The History of Gardens,* London, 1979, p.210), but the Bowood Estate Office believes it was built in the 1820s and moved to its present site in the 1840s.
26. Røstvig, M.-S., *The Happy Man: Studies in the Metamorphosis of a Classical Idea,* 2nd edn., New York, 1971, vol.2, p.42.
27. Shenstone, W., 'Account of an Interview between Shenstone and Thomson', in J.D. Hunt and P. Willis (eds.), *The Genius of the Place,* London, 1975, p.244.
28. Burke, E., *A Philosophical Inquiry into the Origin of our Ideas of the Sublime and the Beautiful,* 1787 edn., London, p.192.
29. Girardin, R.-L., *An Essay on Landscape or On the Means of Improving and Embellising the Country Round our Habitations,* London, 1783, p.149.
30. Loudon, J.C., *Designs for Laying Out of Farms and Farm Buildings in the Scotch Style adapted to England,* London, 1811, p.24.
31. Harris, J., 'The Flower Garden 1730-1830', in J. Harris (ed.), *The Garden: a Celebration of One Thousand Years of British Gardening,* London, 1979.
32. King, R.W., 'The "Ferme Ornée": Philip Southcote and Wooburn Farm', *Garden History Society,* Summer 1974, vol.2, no.3, p.41. The author uses 'Woburn' for the place and 'Wooburn' for the *ferme ornée.*
33. Mallam, D. (ed.), *Letters of William Shenstone,* Minneapolis, 1939, letter of 14 May, 1749.
34. Clark, H.F., *The English Landscape Garden,* London, 1948, p.3.
35. Farrer, R., *On the Eaves of the World,* London, 1917.
36. Clark, H.F., op.cit., p.19.
37. Templeman, W.D., *The Life and Work of William Gilpin 1724-1804,* Illinois Studies in Language and Literature, 1939, vol.24, p.9.
38. Gilpin, W., *Observations on Several Parts of England, particularly the Mountains and Lakes of Cumberland and Westmorland,* London, 1786.
39. Gilpin, W., *Three Essays on Picturesque Beauty, on Picturesque Travel and on Sketching Landscape,* London, 1792, p.57.
40. Ibid., p.8.
41. Price, U., *An essay on the Picturesque, as compared with the Sublime and the Beautiful. . . ,* London, 1794, vol.1, p.9.
42. Ibid., p.10.
43. Burke, E., *An Essay on the Sublime and Beautiful,* 1898 edn., London, p.44.
44. Price, U., op.cit., p.22.
45. Ibid., p.24.
46. Ibid., p.20.
47. Ibid., p.26. The italics in the quotation are the author's.
48. Loudon, J.C. (ed.), *The Landscape Gardening and Landscape Architecture of the Late H. Repton, Esq.,* London, 1840, p.354.
49. Loudon, J.C., *Country Residences,* London, 1806, p.371.
50. Loudon has confused his readers by writing so many books and by changing his mind about styles of garden design. I have attempted to analyse his opinions in 'Loudon's Stylistic Development' in the *Journal of Garden History,* April-June 1982, vol.2, no.2, p.175.
51. *The Quarterly Review,* March 1828, vol.xxxvii, p.316. The article in which the quotation appears is anonymous but it is well known that Scott was the author.
52. Loudon, J.C, *Observations. . . on the Theory and Practice of Landscape Gardening, etc.,* Edinburgh, 1804, p.210.
53. Knight, J.C., *The Landscape, A Didactic Poem,* 2nd edn., London, 1795, p.83.
54. Ibid., p.73.
55. Ibid., p.71.
56. Ibid., p.81.
57. Price, U., op.cit. p.269.
58. Hussey, C., *A Short History of Scotney Castle,* 1963.

Chapter IV (pp.113-165)

1. Pevsner, N., *The Englishness of English Art,* London, 1956, p.168.
2. Ibid., p.181.
3. The style is often described as 'picturesque', with the word used to mean 'like a landscape painting'. The influence of 'picturesque' theory and the Transition Style outside the realm of garden design is discussed in Chapter 6 of Christopher Hussey's *The Picturesque,* London, 1927, and in David Watkin's *The English Vision: The Picturesque in Architecture, Landscape and Garden Design,* London, 1982.

    J. Summerson describes the influence of the theory on the design of Regent Street in Chapter XII of *John Nash: Architect to George IV,* 1949 edn., London. Summerson writes that 'Repton made the "true character" of a landscape his starting-point; Nash did the same with a town, but his "true character" was concerned not with trees, hills, and water, but streets, buildings, and the flow of traffic', p.205.
4. Hunt, J.D., and Willis, P. (eds.), *The Genius of the Place,* London, 1975, p.339.
5. Knight, R.P., *The Landscape,* London, 1794; Price, U., *An Essay on the Picturesque,* London, 1794-8; Repton, H., *Sketches and Hints on Landscape Gardening,* London, 1795.
6. Loudon, J.C. (ed.), *The Landscape Gardening and Landscape Architecture of the Late H. Repton, Esq.,* London, 1840, p.365.
7. Lauder, T.D. (ed.), *Sir Uvedale Price on the Picturesque,* Edinburgh, 1842, pp.297-300.
8. Pevsner, N., *Studies in Art, Architecture and Design,* London, 1969, vol.1, p.145.
9. *Encyclopaedia Britannica,* Edinburgh, 1771, vol.II, p.646. It is possible that Lord Kames was the author of the article.
10. Loudon, J.C. (ed.), op. cit., p.500.

11. Ibid., p.601.
12. Knight, R.P., *Analytical Inquiry,* London, 1808, pp.194-5.
13. Price, U., *An Essay on the Picturesque,* London, 1794-8, chap.2.
14. Knight, R.P., op.cit., p.154.
15. Repton, H.A., *A letter to Sir Uvedale Price Esq.,* London, 1794, p.3.
16. Loudon, J.C. (ed.), op. cit., pp.99-100.
17. Price, U., *A letter to H. Repton Esq.,* London, 1795, p.48.
18. Ibid., p.77.
19. Loudon, J.C. (ed.), op. cit., p.352.
20. Knight, R.P., op.cit., p.85.
21. Price, U., *A letter to H. Repton Esq.,* p.77.
22. Loudon, J.C. (ed.), op. cit., p.352.
23. Ibid., p.196.
24. Ibid., p.61.
25. Ibid., p.183.
26. Repton, H., *An Inquiry into the changes of taste in landscape gardening,* London, 1806, p.138.
27. A full list of Repton's design projects is included in the catalogue to the 1982 Repton exhibition; G. Carter, P. Goode and K. Laurie (eds.), *Humphry Repton, Landscape Gardener, 1752-1818,* 1982.
28. Loudon, J.C. (ed.), op. cit., p.577.
29. Ibid., p.571.
30. M'Intosh, C., *The Book of the Garden,* Edinburgh and London, 1853, vol.1, p.700.
31. Mawson, T.H., *The Art and Craft of Garden Making,* London, 1900, p.124.
32. Turner, T.H.D., 'Loudon's stylistic development', *Journal of Garden History,* April-June 1982, vol.2, no.2.
33. Loudon, J.C., *Encyclopaedia of Gardening,* London, 1822, p.119.
34. Quatremère de Quincy, A.C., *An Essay on the Nature, The End and The Means of Imitation in the Fine Arts,* J.C. Kent (trans.), London, 1837, p.170.
35. Loudon, J.C., *Encyclopaedia of Gardening,* p.1151.
36. Loudon, J.C., *Gardener's Magazine,* 1829, vol.V, p.589.
37. Loudon, J.C., *Encyclopaedia of Cottage, Farm and Villa Architecture,* London, 1842, p.777.
38. Meason, G.L., *On the Landscape Architecture of the Great Painters of Italy,* London, 1828.
39. Hofland, B., *A Descriptive Account of the Mansion and Gardens of White Knights,* London, 1819.
40. Loudon, J.C., *Encyclopaedia of Gardening,* p.1323.
41. Chadwick, G.F., *The Works of Sir Joseph Paxton 1803-1865,* London, 1961.
42. Turner, T.H.D., op. cit.
43. Loudon, J.C., *The Surburban Gardener and Villa Companion,* London, 1838, p.137.
44. Loudon, J.C., *Arboretum et Fruiticetum Britannicum,* 2nd edn., London, 1854, p.200.
45. Loudon, J.C., *The Surburban Gardener and Villa Companion,* p.141.
46. Loudon, J.C., *Gardener's Magazine,* 1834, vol.X, p.559.
47. Loudon, J.C., *The Surburban Gardener and Villa Companion,* p.141.
48. Loudon, J.C., *Self-instruction for Young Gardeners, Foresters, Bailiffs, Land Stewards and Farmers,* London, 1845, p.xxxi.
49. *Annals of Natural History,* May 1839, p.188.
50. Turner, T.H.D., 'John Claudius Loudon and the inception of the public park', *Landscape Design,* Nov. 1982.
51. Loudon, J.C., *Arboretum et Fruiticetum Britannicum,* p.200.
52. Loudon, J.C., *Encyclopaedia of Gardening,* p.904.
53. Loudon, J.C, *Gardener's Magazine,* 1840, vol.XVI, p.622.
54. M'Intosh, C., op.cit., p.594.
55. Loudon, J.C., *Gardener's Magazine,* 1831, vol.VII, p.390.
56. Loudon, J.C., *Encyclopaedia of Cottage, Farm and Villa Architecture,* p.787.
57. Ibid., p.789.
58. Loudon, J.C. (ed.), *The Landscape Gardening and Landscape Architecture of the Late H. Repton, Esq.,* p.525.
59. Ibid., p.536.
60. Ibid., p.552.
61. Kemp, E., *How to Lay Out a Small Garden,* 1864 edn., London, p.120.

Chapter V (pp.166-227)

1. Kemp, E., *How to Lay Out a Small Garden,* 1864 edn., London, p.123.
2. *The Gardener's Chronicle and Agricultural Gazette,* 10 Aug., 1867.
3. Ibid., 29 June, 1867.
4. Ibid., 21 Sept., 1867.
5. Robinson, W., *Gleanings from French Gardens,* London, 1868, p.4.
6. Robinson, W., *The Wild Garden,* 3rd edn., London, 1883, Preface.
7. Hussey, C., *The Life of Sir Edwin Lutyens,* London, 1950, p.83; reprinted Woodbridge 1984.
8. M'Intosh, C., *The Book of the Garden,* Edinburgh and London, 1853, vol. 1, p.663.
9. Hunt, J.D., *The Wider Sea: a life of John Ruskin,* London, 1982, p.59.
10. Cook, E.T., and Wedderburn, A. (eds.), *The Complete Works of John Ruskin,* London, 1903, vol.8, p.140.
11. Robinson, W., *The English Flower Garden,* 13th edn., London, 1921, p.3.
12. Morris, W., *Hopes and Fears for Art,* London, 1882, p.128.
13. Blomfield, R., *The Formal Garden in England,* London, 1892.
14. Sedding, J.D., *Garden Craft Old and New,* London, 1891.
15. Loudon, J.C., *Encyclopaedia of Cottage, Farm and Villa Architecture,* London, 1842, p.2.
16. Jekyll, G., *A Gardener's Testament,* London, 1937, p.33; reprinted Woodbridge 1982.
17. Blomfield wrote in the Preface to the third edition of *The Formal Garden in England,* London, 1901, that 'a somewhat polemical treatment was necessary' but 'the occasion for this no longer exists'. Blomfield was sure about the value of formal gardens and wild gardens. He wrote: 'The object of formal gardening is to bring the two into harmony, to make the house grow out of its surroundings, and to prevent its being an excrescence on the face of nature' (p.2). However he continued to question the value of the middle link in the transition (p.88).

18. Jekyll, G., 'Gardens and Garden Craft', *Edinburgh Review,* July 1896, vol.184, p.180.
19. Sedding, J.D., op.cit., p.118.
20. Jekyll, G., *Wall and Water Gardens,* London, 1901, p.150.
21. Brown, J., *Gardens of a Golden Afternoon. The story of a partnership: Edwin Lutyens and Gertrude Jekyll,* London, 1982, p.103.
22. Hussey, C., op.cit., p.78.
23. Cowley, A., *The Works in Prose and Verse of Mr. A. Cowley with notes by Dr. Hurd,* London, 1809, vol.3, p.173. Cowley was considered the greatest of English poets in his own day.
24. Brown, J., op.cit., chap. 3.
25. Mawson, T.H., *The Art and Craft of Garden Making,* London, 1900, p.3.
26. The *Country Life* book *Gardens Old & New,* 1909, was composed of a series of reprints from the magazine. The date of publication is uncertain. *The Studio* series on *The Gardens of England,* 1907-11, was edited by C. Holme with help from 'Mr. Thomas H. Mawson, Hon. A.R.I.B.A., the distinguished garden-architect'.
27. Sitwell, G., *On the Making of Gardens,* 1909.
28. Hussey, C., op.cit., p.23.
29. Jekyll, G., *Colour Schemes for the Flower Garden,* 1936 edn., reprinted Woodbridge, 1982, p.36.
30. Ibid., p.218.
31. Ibid., p.294.
32. Ibid., preface by T.H.D. Turner, p.11.
33. Lucas-Phillips, C.E., *The New Small Garden,* London, 1979, p.32.
34. Whitehead, G.E., *Garden Design and Construction,* London, 1966, p.13.
35. Morris, W., *News from Nowhere,* London, 1891.
36. Henderson, P. (ed.), *The Letters of William Morris,* London, 1950, letter of 7 Jan., 1882.
37. Robinson, W., *The Wild Garden,* p.18.
38. Robinson, W. (ed.), *Cottage Gardening,* London, vol.1, no.1, 12 Oct., 1892, p.1.
39. Moggridge, H., 'The work of Brenda Colvin', *The Garden,* Nov. 1981, vol.106, pt.II, p.447.
40. Jellicoe, G.A., and Jellicoe, S., *The Landscape of Man,* London, 1975, p.290.
41. Mawson, T.H., *Bolton as it is and as it might be,* London, 1916, p.15.
42. Blomfield, R., *Modernismus,* London, 1934, p.vi.
43. Shepheard, P., *Modern Gardens,* London, 1953. Shepheard acknowledged (p.13) that examples of gardens which are 'inspired by the age in which we live' are 'hard to find'. He suggested that one of the explanations was that 'the garden is itself an ornament' and not susceptible to the functionalist aesthetic.
44. Read, H., *A Concise History of Modern Painting,* 1974 edn., London, p.87.
45. Jaffé, H.L.C., *De Stijl 1917-1931: The Dutch Contribution to Modern Art,* Amsterdam, 1956, p.61.
46. Ibid., p.99.
47. Seligman, J. (trans.), *Theo van Doesburg: Principles of Neoplastic Art,* London, 1969, p.32.
48. Friedman, M., *De Stijl: 1917-1931 Visions of Utopia,* Oxford, 1982, p.149.
49. Crowe, S., *Garden Design,* London, 1958, p.104.
50. Page, R., *The Education of a Gardener,* London, 1962, p.54.
51. Jellicoe, G.A., and Shepherd, J.C., *Italian Gardens of the Renaissance,* London, 1925, p.15.
52. Jellicoe, G.A., and Shepherd, J.C., *Gardens and Design,* London, 1927, p.85.
53. Jellicoe, G.A., 'The Theoretical Planning of Gardens', *Architects' Journal,* 11 Nov., 1931, p.640; 9 Dec., 1931, p.776; 6 Jan., 1932, p.16; 3 Feb., 1932, p.186; 2 May, 1932, p.318; 6 April, 1932, p.472.
54. Jellicoe, G.A., 'Ronald Tree and the Gardens of Ditchley Park', *Garden History,* vol.10, no.1, pp.80-91.
55. Mercer, F.A., *Gardens and Gardening,* London, 1932.
56. Page, R., 'Caves in Landscape Design', *Landscape and Garden,* Autumn 1934, vol.1, no.3.
57. Tunnard, A.C. 'The Influence of Japan on the English Garden', *Landscape and Garden,* Summer 1935, vol.2, no.2, p.49.
58. Tunnard, C., *Gardens in the Modern Landscape,* 2nd edn., London, 1948, p.9.
59. Ibid., p.6.
60. Ibid., p.71.
61. Ibid., p.72.
62. Ibid., p.75.
63. Ibid., p.62.
64. Ibid., p.93. It is ironic that the house at Halland has now been embellished with an Arts and Crafts Style terrace. See Lance Knobel, 'The tragedy of Bentley Wood: How Chermayeff's house has changed', *Architectural Review,* Nov. 1979, vol.CLXVI, no.993, p.310.
65. Ibid., p.94.
66. Naylor, G., *The Bauhaus,* London, 1968, p.9.
67. *Landscape and Garden,* vol.5, no.2, p.101.
68. Hitchcock, H.R., *Modern Architecture in England,* New York, 1937, p.25.
69. Meyer, E.K., 'The Modern Framework', *Landscape Architecture,* March/April 1983, vol.73, no.2, p.50.
70. Tunnard, C., *Gardens in the Modern Landscape,* op.cit., p.8.
71. Aldous, T., and Clouston, B., *Landscape by Design,* London, 1979.
72. Jellicoe, S., and Hurtwood, Lady Allen of, *The Things We See: Gardens,* London, 1953.
73. Crowe, S., op. cit.
74. Ibid., p.12.
75. Ibid., p.138.
76. Alison, A., *Essays on the Nature and Principles of Taste,* 4th edn., London, 1810, p.48.
77. Loudon, J.C., op.cit., p.994.
78. Kemp, E., op.cit., p.306.
79. John Brookes' books include *Room Outside: a plan for the garden,* 1968; *Garden Design and Layout,* 1970; *Living in the Garden,* 1970; *The Small Garden,* 1977.
80. Brookes, J., *Room Outside,* p.41.
81. Jellicoe, G.A., *Studies in Landscape Design,* London, 1960, vol.1. Vol.2 was published in 1966 and vol.3 in 1970.
82. Jellicoe, G.A., and Jellicoe, S., *Modern Private Gardens,* London, 1968, p.10.
83. Jellicoe, G.A., 'Sutton Place: allegory and analogy in the garden'; *Landscape Design,* Oct. 1983, p.9.

84. Tunnard, C., *Gardens in the Modern Landscape,* p.9.
85. Personal letter, 21 Sept., 1983.
86. Ruff, A., *Holland and the Ecological Landscape: recent developments in the approach to urban landscape,* Manchester, 1979.
87. Baines, C., *How to Make a Wildlife Garden,* London, 1985.
88. Stephenson, V., *The Wild Garden,* London, 1985.
89. Cowell, F.R., *The Garden as a Fine Art,* London, 1978.
90. Le Fevre, J., 'Art into Landscape', *Landscape Design,* May 1981, p.34.

91. Creasy, E., *Concrete Toadstools,* Slough, 1979.
92. Harris, J. (ed.), *The Garden: A Celebration of One Thousand Years of British Gardening,* London, 1979, p.4.
93. *Capability Brown and the Northern Landscape,* Tyne and Wear County Council Museums, 1983, p.11.
94. Lancaster, M.L., and Turner, T.H.D., 'The Sun Rises over Liverpool', *Landscape Design,* April 1984, pp.33-5.
95. Lyall, S., 'Teddy Bears' Picnic', *New Society,* May 1984, vol.68, no.1119, pp.184-5.
96. Seligman, J. (trans.), *Theo van Doesburg: Principles of Neoplastic Art,* London, 1969, p.32.

Select Bibliography

Brown, J., *Gardens of a Golden Afternoon. The Story of a partnership: Edwin Lutyens and Gertrude Jekyll,* London, 1982.

Clark, H.F., *The English Landscape Garden,* London, 1948, reprinted 1980.

Hadfield, M., *Gardening in Britain,* London, 1960; revised as *A History of British Gardening,* London, 1969; 3rd edition, London, 1979.

Hadfield, M., Harling R., and Highton L., *British Gardeners: a biographical dictionary,* London, 1980.

Harvey, J., *Medieval Gardens,* London, 1981.

Hunt, J.D., and Willis, P. (eds.), *The Genius of the Place: English Landscape Garden, 1620-1820,* London, 1975, reprinted 1979.

Hussey, C., *English Gardens and Landscapes 1700-1750,* London, 1967.

Hussey, C., *The Picturesque,* London, 1927, reprinted 1967.

Huxley, A., *An Illustrated History of Gardening,* London, 1978.

Jacques, D., *Georgian Gardens: The Reign of Nature,* London, 1983.

Jellicoe, G.A., and Jellicoe, S., *The Landscape of Man,* London, 1975.

Jellicoe, G.A., Jellicoe, S., Goode, P., and Lancaster, M.L., *The Oxford Companion to Gardens,* 1986.

Strong, R., *The Renaissance Garden in England,* London, 1979; paperback, London, 1984.

Stroud, D., *Capability Brown,* London, 1950, reprinted 1957, 1975; paperback 1984.

Stroud, D., *Humphry Repton,* London, 1962.

Thacker, C., *The History of Gardens,* London, 1979.

Thomas, G.S., *Gardens of the National Trust,* London, 1979.

Willis, P., *Charles Bridgeman and the English Landscape Garden,* London, 1977.

Index

(Figures in italics indicate illustration and caption references)

A.A., *see* Architectural Association
Aalto, Alvar, 220-221
Abraham, Robert, 157
Adam and Eve, 9
Addison, Joseph, 14, 30. 37, 43, 83
Aereas, 95
aesthetics, seventeenth century, 20-24
Aiguille de Blatière, France, *120*
Alberti, Leon, 10, 22
Aldous, Tony, 211
Alison, Archibald, 211
Allen, Marjorie, Lady Allen of
    Hurtwood, 211
Alnwick Castle, Northumberland, 98;
    85
Alps, 101, 103; *102*
Alton Towers, Staffordshire, 155-157,
    159, 162, 164, 165; *140, 156-157*
Arcade, Rousham, Oxfordshire, 94;
    93
Architectural Association, 205, 209,
    210
architecture and garden design, 22-23,
    28, 135, 170, 176, 197, 208-210;
    19, 21, 23, 28, 216-217
Aristotle, 21-22, 28
Arp, Jean, 201, 218
Arthur's Seat, Edinburgh, 106
art nouveau, 196, 197; *197*
arts and crafts movement, 37; *see also*
    styles of garden design: Arts and
    Crafts Style
Arts Council, 223
Art Workers' Guild, 170
Ashridge, Hertfordshire, 126, 151,
    159, 165; *158, 160-161*
association, principle of, 116, 121,
    122, 211
Astor, Lord, *186*
Atkinson, William, 135; *134*
Augustan age, *see* styles of garden
    design: Serpentine Style,
    'Augustan' or 'poetic' phase of
Augustus Caesar, 12, 91

Bacchus, 95
Bacon, Francis, 18, 24, 71
Badminton, Gloucestershire, 63
Baines, Chris, *223*
Barillet-Deschamps, Jean-Pierre, 167
Barnbarrow (Barnbarroch), Dumfries
    and Galloway, 108; *106-107*
Barnsley House, Gloucestershire, *71*
Barry, Charles, 135, 139; *138, 142*
Bathurst, Alan, 76, 79
Battersea Park, London, 167
Bauhaus School, 208
Bayham Abbey, Kent, 179; *116*
Beaumont, Guillaume, 73; *57*
Beautiful, the, 41, 104, 114, 115,
    123, 126, 151, 162; *119, 125*
Bedford, Countess of, *see* Harington,
    Lucy

Behai Park, Peking, *227*
Behrens, Peter, 207-208; *206*
Belgians, King of the, *137*
Bell, Quentin, *226*
Belton House, Lincolnshire, *161*
Benson, Robert, *49*
Bentley Wood House, Halland, East
    Sussex, 197, 208, 209, 215;
    207-208
Bicton, Devon, 165
Biddulph Grange, Staffordshire, 165;
    127, 164
Bingham's Melcombe, Dorset, *45*
Birkenhead Park, Cheshire, *111*
Birmingham Botanical Garden, 151;
    147
Blackheath, London, *202*
Blake, Stephen, 70
Blenheim, Oxfordshire, 42, 60, 65,
    90, 98; *33, 43*
Blomfield, Reginald, 170, 172, 173,
    183, 197; *171, 174*
Bodnant, Gwyned, 151
Bonomi, Ignatius, *130*
Boscobel, Shropshire, 46; *45, 50*
Bos Park, Amsterdam, 222-223
Bowes Museum, Barnard Castle,
    136-137
Bowood, Wiltshire, 99; *98-99, 146*
Box Hill, Surrey, 135
Boyceau, Jacques, 23, 71
Bramham Park, West Yorkshire, 75,
    77, 82, 90, 211; *49, 79, 211*
Brancuzi, Constantin, 201
Brant, Sebastian, *11*
Braque, Georges, 200
Brickwall, East Sussex, *174*
Bridgeman, Charles, 60, 62, 63, 79,
    82, 90, 94; *78, 90*
Bridgeman, Sarah, 79; *78*
Brighton Pavilion, East Sussex, 165;
    140-141
'British Worthies', Stowe,
    Buckinghamshire, 94; *85*
Brookes, John, 215; *201, 214-215*
Brown, Jane, 178
Brown, Lancelot 'Capability', 26,
    32-33, 38-42, 60, 79, 82, 83, 95,
    97, 98-99, 104, 112, 116, 126,
    128, 139, 142, 225; *32, 33, 36, 39,
    41, 42, 43, 84-85, 97-99, 106, 138*
Buccleuch, Duke of, *137*
Burke, Edmund, 41, 42, 100, 104,
    123, 124, 225
Burley-on-the-Hill, Leicestershire, *129*
Burlington, Lord, 26, 93, 95
Burne-Jones, Mrs. Edward, 193
Buscot Park, Berkshire, *187*
Bushey Park, Richmond, 63; *44, 61*

Campbell, Colen, 26, 95
Canneel-Claes, Jean, 207; *198*

Cannizaro Park, London, *136-137*
Carlisle, Lord, 86, 95
Cartaret, Lady, 60
Casson, Hugh, 210
Castell, Robert, 27
Castle Drogo, Devon, 179; *179*
Castle Howard, North Yorkshire, 27,
    82, 83, 86, 95, 139; *28, 80, 86-87,
    94*
Caus, Isaac de, 47; *46*
Cézanne, Paul, 198
Chamberlain, D., 181
Chambers, William, 39
Charles I, 12, 49
Charles II, 12, 13, 46, 54, 56, 59, 60,
    79; *45, 50*
Chatsworth, Derbyshire, 40, 64, 99,
    142, 151, 153, 165; *36, 65*
Cheddar Gorge, Somerset, 205; *205*
Chermayeff, Serge, 197, 208
Chevreul, M.E., 155
Chillingham Castle, Northumberland,
    154
Chinese gardens, 18, 30, 39, 40; *144,
    227*
Chiswick House, London, 26, 94, 95;
    19, 84
Christian philosophy, 9-10, 22; *21*
Church, Thomas, 197, 211
Cicero, 94
Cirencester Park, Gloucestershire, 75,
    76, 79; *76*
Civil War, 9, 12, 44, 47, 49, 54;
    11-12, 46, 50
Claremont, Surrey, 94, 205; *42,
    82-83, 137*
Clark, Frank, 103, 210; *102*
Clarke, Kenneth, 30; *29*
classical influences on garden design,
    9, 10, 12, 13, 14, 20-27, 28, 97;
    28-29
Claude (Lorrain), 26, 27, 28, 30, 33,
    104, 111, 115, 116; *29, 118-119*
Cliveden, Buckinghamshire, 139
Clouston, Brian, 211
Coke, Thomas, 64
Colonna, Francesco, 10
Columella, 10, 14
Colvin, Brenda, 195, 215; *212-213*
Commonwealth, The (1649-60), 12,
    54
Commonwealth Institute, London,
    215
conservation gardens, *see* styles of
    garden design: ecological
conservation movement, 113
Constructivism, 198
Cooper, Anthony Ashley, *see*
    Shaftesbury, third Earl of
cottage gardens, 195-196; *196,
    212-213*
Country Life, 181
Cowley, Abraham, 14, 178

Craigmillar Castle, Edinburgh, 106
Creasy, Elizabeth, 225; *225*
Cromwell, Oliver, 12; *50*
Crowe, Sylvia, 211, 215; *211, 214*
Crystal Palace, Sydenham, London, 132, 142, 153, 165; *132, 143*
Cubism, 198, 200, 201, 203; *201*
Cumbernauld, Strathclyde, 211

Dalkeith Palace, Lothian, *137*
D'Argenville, A.J. Dézallier, 16; *16; see also* Le Blond, A.,
Darwin, Charles, 193
Deanery Garden, Berkshire, 178; *178*
Deepdene, Surrey, 135; *134-135*
Derby Arboretum, 149; *148*
Derwent Fells, Lake District, *133*
Derwent, river, 40; *36*
Derwent Water, Lake District, *133*
Descartes, René, 23, 24
De Stijl, 200-201, 211, 222; *198*
Devil's Bridge, St. Gotthard Pass, Switzerland, *102*
Devonshire, Duke of, 142
Ditchley Park, Oxfordshire, 108, 205; *204*
Dobrée, B., 30
Doesburg, Theo van, 200, 226
Dominichino, *130*
Downton Castle, Shropshire, 106, 124; *88-89, 129*
Drayton, Michael, 35
Dryden, John, 23, 28; *31*
Du Fresnoy, C.A., 28
Dumbleton, Gloucestershire, 73; *73*
Duncombe, North Yorkshire, 86, 90; *87*
Duncombe, Thomas, 86
Dutch influence on garden design, 15, 18, 30, 73, 222; *57*

Eckbo, Garrett, 211
Eden, Garden of, 9, 12, 14; *8, 13*
Edinburgh Royal Botanic Garden, 151, 165
Elgood, George S., *192*
Elysian Fields, Stowe, Buckinghamshire, 94; *85*
empiricism, 20, 24-27, 75, 83, 90, 100, 101; *91*
enclosed gardens, *see* styles of garden design: Enclosed Style
Epicurus, 12, 14
Evelyn, John, 14, 56, 59
Expressionism, 198, 203

Fairbrother, Nan, 42
Fanelli, Francesco, *44*
ferme ornée, 7, 83, 99-101, 124, 131; *100; see also* styles of garden design: Serpentine Style, *ferme ornée*
Ferney Hall, Herefordshire, 114
Festival of Britain, 210-211; *210*

Filkins, Oxfordshire, 195-196; *212-213*
Folly Farm, Berkshire, 178; *184*
Fontainebleau, France, 74
forms, Plato's theory of, 20-23, 24, 25, 26, 27, 35, 37, 131, 200; *21, 23*
Fountains Abbey, North Yorkshire, *80*
Four Faces Urn, Bramham Park, West Yorkshire, 211; *77, 211*
Foxley, Herefordshire, 124; *123*

garden design as fine art, 223, 225, 226; *226; see also* landscape painting; modern art
Gardener's Chronicle, The, 167
gardenesque planting, *see* styles of garden design: gardenesque planting
garden festivals, 226; *227*
garden styles, *see* styles of garden design
gardens as symbols of power and influence, 44, 49, 54-56, 59, 76
Gateshead Garden Festival, 226
Gaudie, Antoni, 196
Geddes, Patrick, 34
Genesis, Book of, 9
George I, 74
Gerard, John, 71
Gibberd, Frederick, 211; *210*
Gibson, John, 167
Giekie, A., 35
Gillespie, W., 211
Gilpin, William, 26, 39, 40, 41, 103-104, 106, 114; *39*
Gilpin, William Sawrey, 26, 41; *27*
Girardin, R.-L., 100
Glasgow Garden Festival, 226
Gledstone Hall, North Yorkshire, 179
Glorious Revolution, 12
Glyme, river, 42
Gothein, Marie-Louise, 41
Grand Tour, 95, 103, 106, 131
Gravetye Manor, West Sussex, 168, 172; *172, 177*
Gray, Thomas, 103
Graythwaite Hall, Lake District, *181, 183*
Great Cross Lime Walk, Stowe, Buckinghamshire, 90
Great Dixter, East Sussex, 190, 193; *212*
Great Maytham, Kent, 193
Grecian Vale, Stowe, Buckinghamshire, 95, 98; *84*
Greenwich Park, London, 7, 56, 59-60; *56, 58, 152*
Gropius, Walter, 208
Gruffyed, J. St. Bodfan, *202*
Gwynn, Nell, 59

Haddon Hall, Derbyshire, *51, 171*
Hadrian, 94

Hagley Park, Hereford and Worcester, 211
Halifax, 143; *145*
Halland, East Sussex, *see* Bentley Wood House
Ham House, Richmond, 49, 60, 73
Hamilton, Charles, 95
Hampton Court, Herefordshire, 65-66; *53, 68*
Hampton Court, Richmond, 7, 26, 38, 63, 65; *61-62, 67*
happy husbandsman, 11, 12, 30, 31; *11, 30*
Hardwick Hall, Derbyshire, *150*
Hare Street, Hertfordshire, 124; *125*
Harewood House, West Yorkshire, 99, 108, 139; *92, 105, 138-139*
Harington, Lucy, Countess of Bedford, 47, 66
Harlow, Essex, 211; *210*
Harris, John, 100, 101
Harvey's Store, Guildford, *216*
Hatchlands, Surrey, *117*
Hawksmoor, Nicholas, 86
Heem parks, Holland, 223; *224*
Hemel Hempstead, Hertfordshire, 211
Henderskelf Lane, Castle Howard, North Yorkshire, 83, 86; *87*
Henry VIII, 44
Hepworth Barbara, 201, 218
Hestercombe, Somerset, 178, 193; *184-185*
Hever Castle, Kent, *186-187*
Hicks, Philip, *180*
Hidcote, Gloucestershire, 190, 193; *2*
High Point, Highgate, London, *216-217*
High Wall, Oxford, 225; *226*
Hill, Oliver, 190
Hill, The, Hampstead, London, *188-189*
Hoare, Henry, 95
Hobbes, Thomas, 24
Hogarth, William, 41, 42, 97-98, 225; *96*
Holkham, Norfolk, 139
Homer, 12, 14
Honsholredyk (Honselaarsdijk), The Hague, *52*
Hooker, Joseph, 149, 151
Hoole House, Cheshire, *151*
Hope, Thomas, 135
Horace, 10-12, 13, 14, 27, 28, 32, 76, 83, 91, 99
Hortus conclusus, see styles of garden design: Enclosed Style
Hoskins, W.G., 35, 42
Howard family, 86
Hume, David, 24, 38
Hussey, Christopher, 7, 32, 41, 68, 83, 90, 95, 97, 112, 168, 190; *86*
Huszar, Vilmos, 200
Hyde Park, London, 90; *90*

Institute of Landscape Architects (I.L.A.), 210, 211
Isle of Oxney, 35
Isola Bella, Lake Maggiore, *130*
Italian influence on garden design, 10, 16, 22, 37, 44, 46, 91, 135, 147, 183, 190, 205; *22, 186-190, 204*

Jakobsen, Preben, 220-221; *219, 221-222*
James I, 47
Japanese gardens, 207, 211; *144, 206*
Jekyll, Gertrude, 7, 27, 34, 41, 170, 172-173, 176, 178-179, 190-191, 193, 207, 225; *173, 176, 178, 181, 184-185, 192, 206, 209, 212*
Jellicoe, Geoffrey A., 203, 205, 210, 211, 218; *204-205, 216*
Jellicoe, Susan, 211, 218
Johnson, Hugh, 225
Johnson, Samuel, 23
Johnston, Lawrence, 190
Julius Caesar, 10, 94

Kemp, Edward, 155, 162, 164, 166, 179, 211; *111, 133, 153, 162-163*
Kennedy, George, *146*
Kensington Gardens, London, 63, 65; *62*
Kensington School of Art, 170
Kent, William, 26, 41, 60, 63, 82, 85, 93, 94, 95; *81, 84*
Kenwood, London, *170*
Kew Royal Botanic Garden, London, 139, 149, 151, 165; *142, 196*
Kew Green, *196*
Kiftsgate, Gloucestershire, 190
Kip, J., 66, 72-73, 101; *57, 61, 64-65, 72*
Klee, Paul, 218
Knight, Richard Payne, 38-39, 43, 105-106, 108, 109, 110, 113, 114-116, 121, 122-123, 124, 131, 176, 179, 190, 225; *39, 88-89, 108, 114, 119-120, 122, 129*
knot gardens, *see* styles of garden design: knot gardens
Knyff, Leonard, 65, 66, 72-73, 101; *53, 57, 61, 64-65, 72*

Lake District, 39, 42; *36, 133, 163, 181, 183*
Lambton Castle, Durham, *130*
Lancaster, Michael, *216*
landscape ideal, 30, 32-35, 37, 83, 218; *29*
landscape, interpretation of, 35, 37, 38
landscape painting, 26, 28-30, 99, 104, 115-116, 121, 122; *29, 31, 126; see also* garden design as fine art; modern art

Leasowes, The, 7, 98, 99, 100
Le Blond, Alexander, 71; *70; see also* D'Argenville, A.J. Dézallier
Le Corbusier, 205, 207
Lely, Peter, *15*
Le Nôtre, André, 23, 54, 55, 56, 60, 63; *54, 56*
Leonardslee Gardens, West Sussex, 151; *149*
Leslie, G.D., *183*
Levens Hall, Cumbria, 73, 82; *57, 80*
Leverhulme, Lord, 190; *188, 191*
Liverpool International Garden Festival, 226; *226-227*
Lloyd, Christopher, *212*
Lloyd, Nathaniel, 190
Locke, John, 24-25, 30
London, George, 7, 14, 15, 28, 60, 63, 64, 65, 74, 75, 86; *31, 53, 61, 64, 66, 87*
Loos, Adolf, 207
Longleat, Wiltshire, 65; *64, 117*
Lorrain, *see* Claude
Loudon, J.C., 38, 40, 42, 100, 101, 106, 108, 131, 135, 139, 142, 147, 149, 151, 155, 157, 159, 164, 166, 168, 170, 211; *41, 92, 100, 105-107, 130, 132, 140, 148, 151-153, 155-156, 170*
Louis XIV, 16, 59, 76, 79
Lovejoy, A.O., 7
Lucas-Phillips, C.E., 193
Luton Hoo, Bedfordshire, 98
Lutyens, Edwin, 176, 178-179, 193, 220-221, 225; *176, 178, 181, 184-185, 192*
Luxborough, Lady, 98, 101
Lyall, S., 226

McHarg, Ian, 34
M'Intosh, Charles, 128, 155, 168; *136-137*
Magritte, René, 218
Mall, The, London, 56; *59*
Mallows, C. E., 181
Marly, France, 74
Marx, Burle, 197
Mawson, T.H., 41, 128, 179, 181, 190, 197; *126, 181-183, 188-189, 191, 197*
M.A.R.S., *see* Modern Architecture Research Group
Meason, Gilbert Laing, 135; *134*
Medici, Lorenzo de, 22; *22*
Medici Villa, Careggi, 22; *22*
Melbourne Hall, Derbyshire, 7, 64, 90; *66-67*
Mentmore, Buckinghamshire, 143, 153; *154*
Mereworth Castle, Kent, 26, 95; *19*
Midgeley, K., 193

Miller, Philip, 101
Milton, John, 7, 12, 14; *13*
Miro, Joan, 218
Modern Architecture Research Group (M.A.R.S.), 209-210; *216-217*
modern art, 27, 113, 198, 200-201, 203, 207, 208, 209, 215, 218, 220; *198, 200, 201, 203, 209, 215-217, 219-220; see also* garden design as fine art; landscape painting
Modern Movement in architecture, 196, 197
Moggridge, Hal, 195-196
Mollet, André, 55; *49*
Mollet, Claude, 71
Mollet family, 60, 63
Mondrian, Piet, 200, 201, 215; *198, 215*
Monet, Claude, 218
Montacute, Somerset, *174*
Montegufoni, Italy, 190
Moor Park, Hertfordshire, 18, 47, 49, 66; *17, 47-48, 50*
Moor Park, Surrey, 14, 18, 66, 68-69, 71-72; *68-70*
Moore, Henry, 113, 201, 208, 218; *216-217*
Morris, William, 168, 193
mosaiculture, *see* styles of garden design: floral bedding
Moylan, Karen, *200*
Muir, H., 190
Munstead Wood, Surrey, 7, 178, 193; *176, 192*

Napoleonic Wars, 124-125
Nash, John, 113
National Trust, *2, 32*
nature, imitation of, 18, 20, 21-24, 26, 27, 28, 37, 41, 112, 131, 166, 168; *23*
nature, interpretation of, 20, 21, 23, 24, 25, 26, 27, 35, 37, 38, 168
neo-classicism, 20
neo-plasticism, 198, 201, 203, 218; *201*
Neoplatonism, 20-23, 24, 25, 26, 27, 30, 42, 131, 168, 198
Nesfield, W.A., 139
New Forest, 26; *27*
New Place, Surrey, 193
Newton, Isaac, 155
New Ways, Northampton, 207; *206*
Nicholson, Ben, 218; *220*
Norman conquest, 10
North Sea, 55, 128
North Wales, 104; *103*
Notre-Dame, Paris, 22; *21*
Nourse, Timothy, 30, 42; *30*
Nymans, West Sussex, 151

Old Woodstock Manor, Oxfordshire, 90
Orange, William of, *see* William III
Orchards, Surrey, 178
Osborne, Isle of Wight, 165
Ovid, 14, 28

Page, Russell, 203, 205, 210; *205*
Painshill, Surrey, 95
Palladian architecture, 26, 91; *17, 19, 23, 91*
Palladio, Andrea, 10, 22, 23, 93, 95; *19, 23, 28*
pal-mal, 56, 59; *56*
Panofsky, Erwin, 22
Paradise Lost, 12, *13*
Parc Güell, Barcelona, 196
Parkinson, John, 71; *8, 10*
Parsons, Alfred, *167*
Paston Manor, *16*
Patterson, G., 211
Paxton, Joseph, 139, 142-143, 151, 153; *111, 132, 143, 145, 154*
Penguin Books courtyard, 215; *215*
Penshurst, Kent, 49; *50, 70*
People's Park, Halifax, 143; *145*
Pepys, Samuel, 59
Peto, Harold, 190; *187*
Petworth, West Sussex, 38, 99; *32, 33, 43*
Pevsner, Nikolaus, 15, 42, 113
Picasso, Pablo, 200, 205
Picturesque, the, 39, 90, 103-105, 106, 113, 114-115, 116, 121, 122-123, 124, 151, 179; *118-120, 125*
Piercefield, Monmouthshire, 147; *148*
Pierrepont House, Nottinghamshire, 49; *48*
Plato, 12, 20-21, 22, 24, 25, 37; *22*
Platonic Academy, Florence, 22
Pliny the Younger, 10
Plotinus, 20
Polesden Lacey, Surrey, *128*
Pompey, 94
Pope, Alexander, 14, 23, 24, 25, 68, 76, 79, 82, 91, 93, 113, 121, 211; *25*
Popish Plot, 30
Poussin Gaspar, 95, 111
Poussin, Nicolas, 23, 26, 28, 30, 115, 116, 198; *119*
Powys Castle, Powys, 124; *122*
Price, Uvedale, 33, 39, 40, 43, 104-105, 106, 110-112, 113, 114-116, 121, 122-124, 128, 131, 151, 168, 176, 179, 190; *29, 88, 109-110, 113, 119, 123, 177*
Prior Park, Avon, 98, 124; *97*
Prospect Hill, Longleat, Wiltshire, *117*

Quarterly Review, The, 26
Quatremère de Quincy, A.C., 131
Queen's House, Greenwich Park, London, *56*

Racine, Jean, 23
Raphael, 159
rationalism, 24, 25, 75, 90; *91*
Ray Wood, *see* Wray Wood
recognition, principle of, 147
Regents Park, London, 165
Regent Street, London, 113
Reith Lecture, 113
Renishaw, Derbyshire, 190; *190*
Repton, Humphry, 34, 40, 42, 43, 99, 106, 114-116, 117, 121-124, 126, 128, 131, 151, 155, 159, 162, 165, 173, 176, 179, 190, 225; *36, 88, 115-117, 119, 123, 125, 129, 140, 150, 158, 160-161*
Restoration, 12, 54
Reynolds, Joshua, 23
Rievaulx, North Yorkshire, 86
Robbins, Thomas, 101
Robie house, Chicago, 196
Robinson, William, 27, 166-170, 172, 173, 193-195; 222; *166-167, 169, 171-172, 174-175, 177, 212, 224*
Rocque, John, 56
romanticism, 20, 30
Rosa, Salvator, 101, 103, 111, 115; *102, 118*
Rose, John, 60, 63
Røstvig, Maren-Sofie, 11, 99
Rotherhithe, London, 225
Rothers, river, 35
Round Pond, Kensington Gardens, London, 63
Rousham, Oxfordshire, 90, 94, 124; *81, 93*
Roynton Cottage, Lancashire, 190; *191*
Ruff, Alan, 222
rural retirement, 10-14, 46, 76; *11, 12,*
Ruskin, John, 168, 170; *120*

Sabine Hills, Rome, 12, 83
Sackville-West, Vita, 190; *195*
St. Gotthard Pass, Switzerland, *102*
St. James's Park, London, 30, 56, 59, 60; *56-57*
St. Osyth's Priory, Essex, *51*
St. Paul's Walden Bury, Hertfordshire, 75; *75, 77*
Salmon, William, 35; *31*
Sayes Court, Deptford, 56
Schoenmeakers, M.H.J., 200
Scone Palace, Tayside, 135
Scotney Castle, Kent, 112; *109*
Scott, Walter, 26, 41, 106, 128
Sedding, J.D., 170, 173

Seeger, Stanley, 218
Sefton Park, Liverpool, 165; *165*
Serle, John, *25*
Serpentine, The, Hyde Park, London, 90; *90, 146*
Sezincote, Gloucestershire, 165; *140-141*
Shaftesbury, first Earl of, 25
Shaftesbury, third Earl of (Anthony Ashley Cooper), 14, 15-16, 18, 23, 24, 25-26, 27
Shakespeare, William, 7
Sheen, Richmond, 13
Sheffield Park, East Sussex, 151; *132*
Shendish, Hertfordshire, *162-163*
Shenstone, William, 43, 98, 99-100, 101, 124
Shepheard, Peter, 197, 210; *198, 210*
Shepherd, J.C., 203, 205; *204*
Sheringham Park, Norfolk, 126, 128; *125, 129*
Shrewsbury, Earl of, 157, 159, 162
Shrewsbury, Elizabeth, *150*
Shrubland, Suffolk, 139; *142*
Shugborough, Staffordshire, 164, 165
Sissinghurst, Kent, 190, 193; *194-195*
Sitwell, George, 183, 190; *190*
Sitwell, Sacheverell, 42
Somerset House, London, *44*
Sorensen, C. Th., 211, 221
Southcote, Philip, 99
Stanley Park, Liverpool, *153*
Steuart, Henry, 26; *27*
Stevenage, Hertfordshire, 211
Stoke-on-Trent Garden Festival, 226
Stonehenge, 157; *156*
Stourhead, Wiltshire, 26, 90, 95, 124; *90*
Stowe, Buckinghamshire, 40, 79, 82, 90, 94, 95; *78, 84-85, 91*
Stowe, John, *59*
Strabbo, Abbot, 44
Strong, Roy, 44, 46, 47
Stroud, Dorothy, 32, 41, 98
Studio, The, 41, 181, 205; *204*
Studley Royal, 82, 90; *80, 91*
styles of garden design, 37, 42-43 (entries with capital letters denote the eleven main styles identified by the author)
   Abstract Style, 196-211, 215-220, 226; *198-208, 210-211, 214-217, 219-222*
   Arts and Crafts Style, 166-196, 203, 220, 225; *166-167, 169-192, 194-196, 212*
   Dutch Style, 15, 54-55, 63-73, 75, 79; *37, 52-53, 55, 57, 63-69, 72-73, 78*
   eclectic, 44, 47
   ecological, 221-224; *223-224*
   emblematic, 44

continued

styles of garden design *(continued)*
  Enclosed Style, 42, 44-51, 56, 72, 114; *30, 44-48, 50-51*
  floral bedding, 151-155, 168; *136-137, 150-154, 170*
  Forest Style, 63, 74-82, 83, 94, 114, 222; *37, 74-80, 224*
  French Style, 15, 16, 24, 54-63, 73, 75, 76; *25, 49, 52, 54-59, 61-62*
  gardenesque planting, 147-149, 151, 155; *132, 147-149*
  heraldic, 44
  Irregular Style, 101-112, 114, 124, 170, 222, 224; *37, 88-89, 92, 105, 107-112, 129, 172*
  Italian Style, 128, 130, 131, 134, 135, 139, 142-143; *130, 134-135, 138-139, 142-143, 145, 146*
  knot gardens, 71; *45, 70-71*
  mannerist, 44
  Mixed Style, 144, 155-165, 226; *127, 133, 140-141, 155-158, 160-165, 227*
  Serpentine Style, 63, 82-87, 90-91, 93-101; *37, 80-87, 90-91, 93-101, 105*
    'Augustan' or 'poetic' phase of, 91, 93-95; *82-85, 91, 93*
    'Brownian' or 'abstract' phase of, 83, 95, 97-99; *96-99*
    ferme ornée, 83, 99-101; *100*
  Transition Style, 37, 113-129, 135, 139, 151, 170, 172-173; *37, 116-120, 125-129*
  Victorian planting, 147-155; *136-137, 140-141, 145, 147-154*
Sublime, the, 101, 104, 113, 114-115, 123, 128, 143; *36, 118-119, 125, 132-133*
Sutherland, Graham, 218
Sutton Place, Surrey, 218; *220*
Switzer, Stephen, 14-16, 18, 24, 32, 60, 63, 74-75, 76, 79, 82, 86, 99; *16*

Tatton Park, Cheshire, 164, 165; *144*
Tecton, *216*
Temple of Ancient Virtue, Stowe, Buckinghamshire, 94; *85*
Temple, Dorothy, 66, 72

Temple of Flora, Stourhead, Wiltshire, 95
Temple of Four Winds, Castle Howard, North Yorkshire, 27, 86, 95; *28*
Temple of Vesta, Tivoli, Italy, 27, 94; *28*
Temple, William, 13-15, 18, 24, 30, 47, 49, 66, 68, 71; *15, 17, 48, 50, 68, 70*
Teniers, David, 159
Tew Lodge, Oxfordshire, 7, 100, 101; *100*
theme gardens, 226; *227*
theme park, 159
Theocritus, 12
Thijsse (J.P.) Park, Holland, 223; *224*
Thomas, Inigo, 190
Thomas, John, *146*
Tipping, H.A., 190
Tivoli gorge, Italy, 94
Trafalgar Square, London, 139
Transport, Minstry of, 7
Tree, Ronald, 203, 205
Trentham, Staffordshire, 135, 139; *138*
Triggs, H. Inigo, 183; *66*
Triple Alliance, 13
Troy, 95
Tunnard, Christopher, 197, 205, 207-208, 209, 210, 211, 218; *206-208*
Turner, J.M.W., 7, 26, 38, 99, 193
Tynningham, Lothian, 62
Tyringham, Buckinghamshire, 179

Underscar, Lake District, *133, 163*
University College, London, 210

Valleyfield, Fife, 151; *150*
Vanbrugh, John, 42, 65, 86, 90; *28*
Vaux-le-Vicomte, France, 54, 55
Venus Vale, Rousham, Oxfordshire, 94; *93*
Versailles, France, 16, 54, 55, 59, 60, 74, 76, 79, 142; *54*
Villa Capra, Vicenza, 95; *19, 23, 28*
Villa d'Este, Italy, 173; *173*
Virgil, 10-12, 14, 27, 28, 32, 34, 71, 91, 95; *11, 13, 31*
Vitruvius, 10, 14, 179
Vorstermans, J., *56*

Waddesdon Manor, Buckinghamshire, 165
Wakehurst Place, West Sussex, 151; *148*
Walpole, Horace, 37, 38, 39, 93, 94, 103
Warwick Priory, Warwickshire, 65
Wasdale Head, Lake District, *36*
Water of Leith, Edinburgh, 106
Watkin, David, 7
Watteau, Antoine, 115; *119*
Watts, William, 101; *101*
Westbury Court, Gloucestershire, 73; *73*
Wexham Springs, Buckinghamshire, 215; *199, 214*
Whatley, Thomas, 38
Whitehead, Alfred North, 21
Whitehead, G.E, 193
William III, 13, 54
Willis, P., 79
Wilson, James, 130
Wilson, R., 26
Wilton, Wiltshire, *46*
Wimbledon House, Merton, London, 155
Wimborne St. Giles, Dorset, 18
Windsor Forest, 76
Wingerworth, Derby, 124; *123*
Winterbourne, Birmingham, 165; *144*
Wise, Henry, 7, 14, 15, 60, 63, 64, 65, 74, 75; *53, 61, 62, 66*
Wittkower, R., 22
Woburn Abbey, Bedfordshire, 151, 159, 165
Woburn Farm, Surrey, 99, 101
Wood House, Devon, *182*
Wood, John, *49*
Wotton, H., 18
Wordsworth, William, 82
World, The, 97
Wray Wood, Castle Howard, North Yorkshire, 83, 86, 95; *86*
Wrest Park, Bedfordshire, 74, 75; *74*
Wright, Frank Lloyd, 196, 203, 205
Wyatt, Katherine Montagu, *192*
Wyatville, Jeffry, 142
Wye, river, 104
Wye Valley, 39; *148*

Youngman, Peter, 210, 211

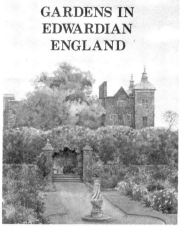

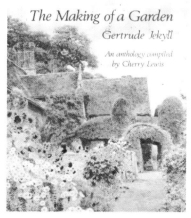